To whom shall I dedicate this book?

A. To my beautiful boys, Arlo and Alby
B. To my gorgeous Granma Elizabeth
C. To my wonderful god-daughters, Eleanor, Faye and Livia
D. To curious children of all ages

Answer: All of the above!

LADYBIRD BOOKS

Ladybird Books is part of the Penguin Random House group of companies
whose addresses can be found at global.penguinrandomhouse.com.
www.penguin.co.uk   www.puffin.co.uk   www.ladybird.co.uk

Penguin
Random House
UK

First published 2024
001
Text copyright © Molly Oldfield, 2024
Illustrations copyright © Ladybird Books Ltd, 2021, 2024
The moral right of the author has been asserted

Parts of this book previously published in the *Guardian*.
Copyright © Guardian News & Media Ltd and Molly Oldfield, 2021–2024

Set in 12/14.5pt Avenir LT Pro
Typeset by Jouve (UK), Milton Keynes
Printed and bound in Great Britain by Clays Ltd, Elcograf S.p.A.

The authorized representative in the EEA is Penguin Random House Ireland,
Morrison Chambers, 32 Nassau Street, Dublin D02 YH68

A CIP catalogue record for this book is available from the British Library

ISBN: 978–0–241–70383–0

All correspondence to:
Ladybird Books, Penguin Random House Children's
One Embassy Gardens, 8 Viaduct Gardens, London SW11 7BW

MOLLY OLDFIELD

EVERYTHING UNDER THE SUN

QUIZ BOOK

MOLLY OLDFIELD is the host of
Everything Under the Sun, a podcast that answers
questions from children around the world. The aim
of the podcast is to make sure that no child's
curiosity or questions go unanswered again!

Molly believes that the more curious you are,
the more adventurous your life will be – and there's
so much to learn about everything under the sun!

Molly is the author of *The Secret Museum*,
Wonders of the World's Museums,
Natural Wonders of the World and the
bestselling book *Everything Under the Sun*.

Molly has two beautiful boys and loves going
on adventures with her family. She wrote this
book while living in Bali with her children, which
is why the first question is about bamboo!

For more information about the podcast,
including how to listen and how to send in
your own questions, go to www.mollyoldfield.co.uk

Other Ladybird books by Molly Oldfield
Everything Under the Sun:
A curious question for every day of the year

CONTENTS

INTRODUCTION

Hello, and welcome to the
Everything Under the Sun Quiz Book!

I'm Molly, and each week I make a podcast
for children. It's called *Everything Under the Sun*,
and kids from all over the world send me their
questions about anything and everything.

What is the biggest species
of bamboo in the world?
How many babies are born each day?
How do sharks clean their teeth?
Are there rainbows on other planets?
Is there sunken treasure in the ocean?
Why do wombats have pouches?

I love hearing all these curious questions!
And, usually, I answer them with the help
of an expert. This time, though, I thought
it would be fun to give YOU the chance
to try to answer them first.

For every question in this book, there are
three possible answers to choose from.
Pick the one you think is correct . . . then turn to
the answers section at the back of the book
to find out whether you got it right!

You can play by yourself or with your
friends, family, teachers or anyone you
love to hang out with.

There are 366 questions – one for every day
of the year, plus a bonus leap-year question –
and they are on all kinds of subjects . . .
Everything under the sun!

Thanks for reading and enjoy!

Love from

Molly

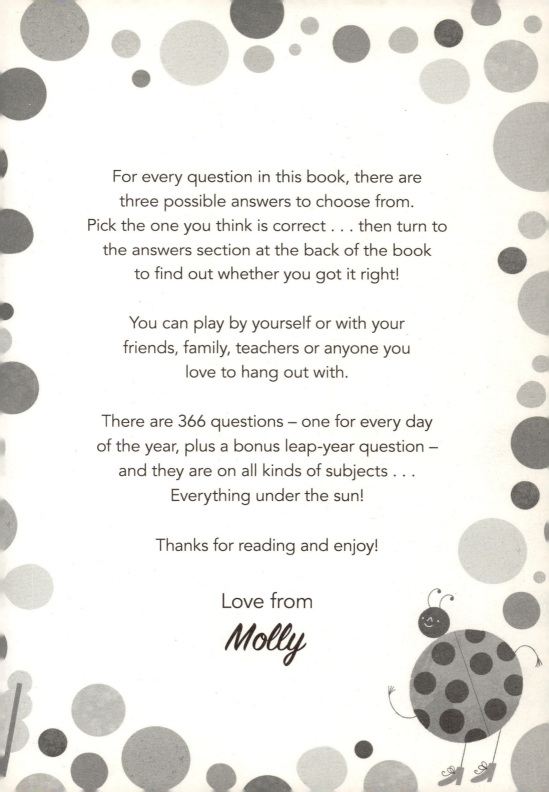

QUESTIONS

1 WHAT IS THE BIGGEST BAMBOO IN THE WORLD?

A Giant dragon bamboo

B Giant panda bamboo

C Giant ape bamboo

2 HOW MANY HUMAN BABIES ARE BORN EVERY DAY?

A About 215,000

B About 385,000

C About 575,000

3 WHAT DOES THE MOON SMELL LIKE?

A Cheese

B Nothing

C Gunpowder

4 WHAT COLOUR IS THE MOON?

A Yellow

B Blue

C Grey

5 HOW BIG IS THE MOON?

A If the Earth were a tennis ball, the Moon would be a marble

B If the Earth were a tennis ball, the Moon would be a baseball

C If the Earth were a tennis ball, the Moon would be a basketball

6 HOW MANY GRAINS OF SAND ARE THERE ON EARTH?

A 7 quintillion 500 quadrillion

B 1 billion million trillion

C 41 quadrillion

7 ARE THERE RAINBOWS ON OTHER PLANETS?

A Only on Jupiter

B Yes, every planet gets rainbows

C So far, Earth is the only planet we know of to experience the joy of rainbows

8 IF YOU DUG FROM ENGLAND THROUGH THE EARTH, WOULD YOU REALLY GET TO AUSTRALIA?

A Yes, because England is directly opposite Australia

B No, because England is directly opposite Hawai'i

C No, because England is directly opposite the Pacific Ocean, south of New Zealand

9 WHAT DO KANGAROOS LIKE TO EAT?

A They eat meat

B They love to eat barbecued shrimps (otherwise known as prawns)

C They are herbivores and mostly eat plants

10 WHY DOES CHLORINE HAVE TO BE IN SWIMMING POOLS?

A To kill germs

B To stop fish moving in

C So that the pools smell funny and ducks won't want to swim in them

11 WHY DO COWS HAVE FOUR STOMACHS?

A Because they eat four times as much as humans do

B No one knows! They have four stomachs, but actually use only one

C They don't! Cows have only one stomach

12 WHY ARE COW FARTS SO BAD FOR THE ENVIRONMENT?

A They're not actually that bad!

B Because they're super stinky and make the Earth smell disgusting

C Because they can catch alight and start wildfires

13 WHY DOES THE WORLD SPIN?

A Because the Earth was hit by an asteroid

B Because it's heavier on one side than the other

C Because the Sun pulls it along, and the Sun spins

14 HOW MANY EARTHS COULD YOU FIT INSIDE THE SUN?

A 1.3 million

B 250,000

C One – the Earth and the Sun are the same size

15 WHY DOES THE EARTH SPIN ROUND WITHOUT US FEELING IT?

A   We move with it, and so does everything around us, so we don't feel or notice it

B   When we are born, our brains are programmed not to feel the movement

C   It doesn't spin – it's the sky that spins! That's why we see stars, the Moon and the Sun moving across the sky

16 HOW HOT IS THE SUN?

A   As hot as a pitta bread that has just been toasted

B   As hot as a volcano's lava

C   It depends where you measure it, but the core is 15 million degrees Celsius.

17 WHAT IS THE SMALLEST BIRD THAT CANNOT FLY?

A The Inaccessible Island rail

B The kākāpō

C The chicken

18 WHY DO BIRDS HAVE FEATHERS?

A So that they feel soft and fluffy

B To give humans something to write with before pens and pencils were invented

C To help them to fly, to keep warm and dry, and to show off (or to blend in)

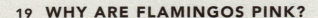

19 WHY ARE FLAMINGOS PINK?

A Because they eat too many pink ice lollies

B Because they colour in their feathers with pink paint

C Because their food turns them pink

20 WHAT IS THE DEMON DUCK OF DOOM?

A A giant duck-like bird that couldn't fly and roamed Australia over 65,000 years ago

B A giant duck that escaped from hell and now causes trouble in small ponds

C A tiny duck that is really naughty and pokes other ducks with its beak

21 WHAT SOUND DOES A CASSOWARY MAKE?

A   A deep growl

B   A high-pitched squawk

C   A chirping squeak

22 WHAT IS THE BIGGEST COUNTRY IN THE WORLD?

A   Russia

B   India

C   Canada

23 WHAT DID PEOPLE DO ALL DAY IN ANCIENT EGYPT?

A The only thing you could do in ancient Egypt was build pyramids

B Most people were farmers

C We know nothing about ancient Egyptians – their life is a mystery

24 WHAT WERE THE BIGGEST DINOSAURS?

A Titanosaurs

B Gigantosaurs

C Humungosaurs

25 WHAT WAS THE VERY FIRST DINOSAUR?

A *Tyrannosaurus rex*

B *Diplodocus*

C *Nyasasaurus*

26 HOW DID DINOSAURS BECOME EXTINCT?

A Because the world got too cold for them to survive

B Because an asteroid hit the Earth

C Because they were eaten by top predators

27 WHERE DID DINOSAURS LIVE?

A Only in Africa

B Mostly in Asia

C In our imaginations

28 WHAT IS THE SMALLEST PLANET IN OUR SOLAR SYSTEM?

A Neptune

B Venus

C Mercury

29 WHAT IS IN THE MIDDLE OF THE PLANET MARS?

A Iron, nickel and sulphur

B Caramel and nougat

C Stone, iron and bronze

30 WHAT IS THE CLOSEST STAR TO EARTH?

A The Sun

B Alpha Centauri

C The North Star

31 HOW DO CLOUDS FLOAT IN THE SKY?

A They're made of candy floss, which is very light

B They're held on strings from the sky

C They're made from tiny water droplets, which are very light

1 WHAT IS IT LIKE INSIDE A CHRYSALIS?

A It is full of sparkling colours, so the caterpillar can become a butterfly and cover its wings in colours

B It is full of caterpillar soup, or liquid caterpillar

C It is full of flowers to feed the caterpillar as it turns into a butterfly

2 HOW DO BUTTERFLIES TASTE WITH THEIR FEET?

A They have tongues with tiny tastebuds on their feet

B They have taste receptors called chemoreceptors on their feet

C They have tiny caterpillars on their feet that taste things for them

3 WHAT DO BUTTERFLIES EAT?

A Butterfly-pea flowers

B Chocolate

C Nectar, blood, sweat and poop

4 WHY DO BUTTERFLIES HAVE DIFFERENT COLOURS ON THEIR WINGS?

A To protect them and to help them find a mate

B Because they are very vain and need to be colourful to feel beautiful

C To make them easier to see when they're flying

5 WHY ARE WE TICKLISH?

A So that we laugh more, because laughing is good for us

B Because we evolved from monkeys, and monkeys use tickling as a way to communicate

C It's a defence mechanism

6 WHAT MAKES US HICCUP?

A Eating or drinking too much, or too quickly

B Being boiling hot and needing to breathe in cool air quickly

C Being very excited

7 WHY CAN I MAKE SHAPES WITH MY TONGUE AND OTHER PEOPLE CAN'T?

A It takes practice! Practice makes perfect

B The tongue-rolling skill gets passed down in your family – if your parents can do it, the chances are you can, too!

C It depends on the size and shape of your tongue

8 WHY DO OUR NOSES RUN IN COLD WEATHER?

A Because cold weather makes us catch a cold, so we produce more snot

B To keep the inside of our noses moist, so they don't get irritated by the cold air

C Because cold weather makes our skin get thinner, so we leak more fluids

9 WHY DO PEOPLE GIVE RED ENVELOPES AT LUNAR NEW YEAR?

A Because red represents energy and fortune, and the envelopes are full of money

B Because red is the colour of the sunrise, so it's showing it's the start of a new year

C Because red is the colour your cheeks go when you're shy, and giving presents sometimes makes people feel shy

10 HOW MANY ANIMALS ARE THERE IN THE CHINESE ZODIAC?

A 30

B Ten

C Twelve

11 WHY DO WE SOMETIMES SEND LANTERNS INTO THE SKY FOR LUNAR NEW YEAR?

A   To celebrate hope, letting go and a happy future

B   To deliver letters to friends who live far away

C   To send away all the annoying things that happened in the last year

12 WHY DID THE ANCIENT EGYPTIANS WRAP MUMMIES IN BANDAGES?

A   To keep them warm

B   To make them look scary

C   To protect the body so it could be used again in the afterlife

13 WHY DO CARS KEEP MOVING?

A Because drivers move them with their minds

B Because the driver presses their foot down on the accelerator, which sends energy along to the wheels and makes them go round, moving the car

C Because they're pushed along by the wind

14 WHY DO CARS HAVE LOTS OF PIPES?

A To give the car as much fuel as possible!

B Because pipes look cool and powerful

C To give the car important liquids and gases, and to get rid of fumes

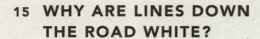

15 WHY ARE LINES DOWN THE ROAD WHITE?

A The idea came from seeing milk spilled on the road

B Because they were originally drawn with white chalk, and the white stuck

C Because white is the easiest colour to see against dark roads

16 WHAT IS THE ONLY MAMMAL THAT CANNOT FART?

A A sloth

B A whale

C A hedgehog

17 HOW DO SKUNKS GET THEIR SMELL OUT?

A   By shooting stinky spray out of their feet

B   By breathing out a terrible stench

C   By shooting stinky spray out of glands on each side of their bottoms

18 WHY DO FARTS SMELL?

A   Often they don't! But the ones that do contain hydrogen sulphide

B   Because it's your body's way of scaring people off

C   They only smell when you have eaten too many eggs

19 DO HURRICANES ALWAYS SPIN IN THE SAME DIRECTION?

A Yes, they always spin clockwise – in the opposite direction from the way the Earth spins

B Yes, they always spin counterclockwise – in the same direction as the Earth spins

C No, they spin counterclockwise in the northern hemisphere, and clockwise in the southern hemisphere

20 HOW DO WEATHER FORECASTERS PREDICT THE WEATHER?

A By using satellites and supercomputers

B By looking out of the window

C By asking people on the International Space Station to tell them where storms are heading

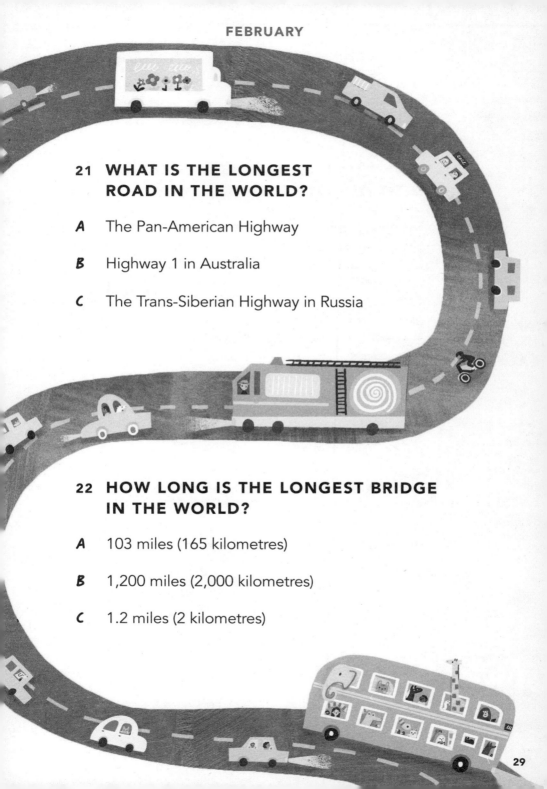

21 WHAT IS THE LONGEST ROAD IN THE WORLD?

A The Pan-American Highway

B Highway 1 in Australia

C The Trans-Siberian Highway in Russia

22 HOW LONG IS THE LONGEST BRIDGE IN THE WORLD?

A 103 miles (165 kilometres)

B 1,200 miles (2,000 kilometres)

C 1.2 miles (2 kilometres)

23 WHY DON'T OUR EYEBALLS FALL INTO OUR BODIES?

A Because they are glued into the eye socket

B Our eyeballs CAN fall into our bodies – watch out!

C Because they are held in place by the optic nerve and the bone in the eye socket

24 WHY DO ONIONS MAKE OUR EYES WATER?

A Because our eyes feel really sad when we cut an onion

B Because our eyes think onion tastes disgusting

C To make tears to wash out a harmful chemical made by cutting up onions

25 WHY ARE TEARS SALTY?

A Because all the fluids in our bodies contain a little salt, including tears, sweat and saliva

B So that you can taste yourself crying

C Because they are made out of seawater

26 CAN YOU CRY UNDERWATER?

A Yes

B No, there is too much water around your eyes for tears to form

C You can't cry one tear – but, if you cry hard enough, lots of tears will come out

27 WHICH ANIMAL HAS THE MOST EYES?

A All animals have two eyes, because it is the best way to be able to see well

B Lizards

C Scallops

28 WHO MADE UP THE "HAPPY BIRTHDAY" SONG?

A No one has any idea!

B A seven-year-old in Melbourne, in Australia

C Two people in Kentucky, in the United States of America

29 WHY DO WE HAVE LEAP YEARS?

A Because of the time it takes the Earth to orbit the Sun

B To give us all an extra day of holiday every four years

C Because of the time it takes for the Moon to orbit the Earth

1 HOW DO PHONES PICK UP TEXT MESSAGES WITHOUT WIRES?

A It's magic!

B One phone turns the text into digital data, which is turned into a radio wave, which is sent to a Wi-Fi router, which sends the wave to another phone, which turns it back into text!

C The text messages are carried by wind in the air

2 HOW DO TELEVISION REMOTE CONTROLS WORK?

A By using infrared or radio frequency

B Little goblins inside the remote shout at the TV to tell it what to do

C By sending sounds to tell the TV what to do

3 WHAT WAS THE FIRST GAMES CONSOLE?

A The Nintendo 64

B The Megatron Jumper

C The Magnavox Odyssey

4 CAN DOGS MAKE WOOL?

A No, wool can only be made from sheep

B Yes, wool can be made from any animal

C Yes, wool can be made from sheep, rabbits, goats, alpacas and even a species of dog!

5 WHY DO DOGS HAVE FUR?

A So that they are soft to stroke

B So that they can drop hair all over the place and let other dogs know where they have been

C To control their body temperature, and protect them from cuts and scratches

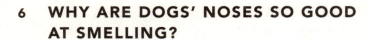

6 WHY ARE DOGS' NOSES SO GOOD AT SMELLING?

A Because their noses and brains are highly sensitive to smell

B Because their noses are all wet, which means that smells stick to them

C Because they spend a lot of time training when they're puppies to develop powerful noses

7 WHAT IS THE SCIENTIFIC NAME FOR A FOXGLOVE?

A *Gladioli foxilis*

B *Foxglovius maximus*

C *Digitalis*

8 WHAT WAS THE FIRST FLOWER?

A A rose

B An apple blossom

C A white flower that looked a bit like a water lily mixed with a magnolia

9 HOW MANY SEEDS ARE THERE IN ONE SUNFLOWER?

A 100

B 2,000

C One million

10 IS THERE AN ANIMAL CALLED A DUMBLEDORE?

A No, only a famous wizard!

B Yes, it's another word for a bumblebee

C Yes, it's a type of elephant with really big ears

11 WHERE DID BANANAS FIRST GROW?

A The Amazon rainforest

B Madagascar

C Malaysia, Indonesia and the Philippines

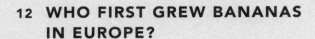

12 WHO FIRST GREW BANANAS IN EUROPE?

A A woman who lived in the Brecon Beacons, in Wales

B A man from Leicestershire, in England, called Mr Sananas

C A Swedish scientist, botanist and explorer called Carl Linnaeus

13 WHAT IS OUR APPENDIX FOR?

A Digesting apple pips we swallow by accident

B Helping to fight infection

C Breaking down chewy food

14 IF YOU DREW A LINE WITH A BIRO UNTIL IT RAN OUT, HOW LONG WOULD THE LINE BE?

A   2 miles (3 kilometres) – the length of 125 tennis courts

B   25 metres – the length of a blue whale

C   50 metres – the length of an Olympic-size swimming pool

15 WHY DO HELIUM BALLOONS FLOAT?

A   Because they're pulled upwards by the Sun

B   Because they aren't affected by gravity

C   Because helium is lighter than air

16 WHY DO WE GROW HAIR IN OUR ARMPITS?

A To keep them warm

B To stop our skin rubbing and getting sore

C It helps to attract a mate

17 WHY DO PEOPLE VOMIT?

A It's the body's way of getting rid of things that could do them harm

B Because they're fed up and want to go home

C Because they're super tired and need to sleep

18 WHY IS BLOOD RED?

A Because it is hot

B Because it turns red in sunlight

C Because it contains something called heme, which is red

19 HOW MANY BLOOD CELLS ARE THERE IN YOUR BODY?

A 35 million

B 35 billion

C 35 trillion

20 HOW FAR DO OUR BLOOD VESSELS STRETCH?

A 3,462 miles (5,572 kilometres) – the same as from London to New York

B 60,000 miles (96,560 kilometres) – the same as from London all the way round the Earth 2.4 times

C 238,855 miles (384,400 kilometres) – the same as from London to the Moon

21 WHICH BREED OF DOG CAN RUN THE FASTEST?

A A wolfhound

B A greyhound

C A whippet

22 WHY DO DOGS HAVE TAILS?

A   To make them look cute to other dogs

B   To balance, move and communicate

C   To cushion their bottoms when they sit down

23 HOW MANY ANTS LIVE IN ONE COLONY?

A   Just two

B   One million

C   Billions!

24 WHAT SOUNDS DO TURTLES MAKE?

A They sing long, deep songs that can travel for miles through the oceans

B The only sound we hear from them is heavy breathing

C They blow bubbles that make a bubbling sound

25 HOW CAN YOU TELL THE DIFFERENCE BETWEEN A MALE AND A FEMALE TURTLE?

A You can't – they look identical

B Females have lighter shells

C Males have longer tails

26 WHICH ANIMAL DOESN'T SLEEP?

A A jaguar

B All creatures need to sleep

C An owl

27 HOW HEAVY IS THE KING'S IMPERIAL STATE CROWN?

A 1 kilogram – about the same as a pineapple

B 2 kilograms – about the same as a bag of twelve apples

C 5 kilograms – about the same as five bags of sugar

28 WHO WAS THE LONGEST-REIGNING BRITISH MONARCH?

A Queen Victoria

B Queen Elizabeth II

C King Henry VIII

29 HOW HIGH CAN A GUINEA PIG JUMP?

A 24 centimetres

B 2 centimetres

C 100 centimetres

30 WHY ARE HAMSTERS ILLEGAL IN HAWAI'I?

A Because their name starts with H and Hawai'i said, "Stop copying me!"

B Because they have so many babies they could spread too quickly and threaten the local animals

C Because a hamster once escaped and killed 20 humans!

31 WHY DO PIGS ROLL IN MUD?

A Because it helps them to keep cool

B So that other pigs can't see them

C Because they love the feeling of the squidgy mud

1 WHAT WAS THE WORLD'S HEAVIEST CHOCOLATE BAR?

A A giant white-chocolate bar in Switzerland shaped like a cow

B A giant chocolate bar with a huge golden ticket inside the wrapper

C A milk-chocolate bar in Derbyshire, in England

2 HOW DO YOU MAKE CHOCOLATE SPREAD?

A First, roast some hazelnuts, then blend them into butter, and add cocoa powder and chocolate

B Find a chocolate bar and let it melt in the sun

C Mix chocolate powder with butter and jam

3 WHICH COUNTRY MAKES THE MOST CHOCOLATE?

A Mexico

B Germany

C Switzerland

4 WHO MADE THE FIRST CHOCOLATE BAR?

A Willy Wonka

B Joseph Fry

C The Easter Bunny

5 DO REPTILES CRY?

A Yes, they cry when they're sad or emotional, just like humans do

B Yes, but only to clear out their eyes and protect them, not because they're sad

C No, reptiles prefer to bite when they're emotional

6 WHERE DO CROCODILES LIVE?

A In the River Thames in England

B In many parts of the world, including Africa, Asia, Australia and the Americas

C Wherever there are rivers

7 WHERE IN THE WORLD ARE YOU MOST LIKELY TO MEET A CROCODILE?

A The Tárcoles River in Central America

B The Amazon River in South America

C The Zambezi River in Africa

8 WHICH ANIMALS HAVE THE LONGEST CLAWS?

A Armadillos

B Crocodiles

C Wild cats

9 HOW MANY BREATHS DO WE TAKE EACH DAY?

A 20,000

B 2,000

C 200

10 CAN BABIES SPEAK SIGN LANGUAGE?

A No, they're much too small

B Some can, but only the really clever ones

C Yes, they can be taught baby sign language when they're around six months old

11 WHY DOESN'T THE MOON FALL OUT OF THE SKY?

A   It is stuck there with superglue

B   Gravity and speed keep it in place

C   There's an alien who lives between the Moon and the Earth and keeps the two perfectly spaced apart

12 HOW DO BATS LOOK AFTER THEIR BABIES IF THEY'RE UPSIDE DOWN?

A   They don't stay upside down – they turn the other way round when they have babies and stay that way until their babies are adults

B   They have upside-down pouches on their tummies that their babies live in

C   They give birth to their babies upside down and catch the babies in their wings, then the babies cling on to them

13 WHY ARE BATS BLIND?

A They aren't – they can actually see very well, thank you

B Because they use sound to navigate, so they don't need to be able to see

C They aren't, but since they have such incredible hearing they can only see a tiny bit

14 HOW OLD CAN AN ANGLERFISH LIVE TO?

A 2.5 years

B 25 years

C 250 years

15 WHICH OCEAN IS THE OLDEST?

A The Atlantic

B The Pacific

C The Indian

16 WHAT IS THE FASTEST MAMMAL IN THE OCEAN?

A The blue whale

B The orca

C The common dolphin

17 HOW TALL IS THE BIGGEST COAST REDWOOD TREE?

A 116 metres – nearly as tall as the Centre Point building in London, in England

B 111 metres – as tall as St Paul's Cathedral in London, in England

C 93 metres – as tall as the Statue of Liberty (including its pedestal!) in New York, in the United States of America

18 HOW DO TREES TURN CARBON INTO CLEAN AIR?

A They suck in carbon, wash it in their trunks, then release clean air through their roots

B They pull carbon dioxide out of the air, do something incredible called photosynthesis, then release oxygen

C They suck carbon out of the soil, clean it in their roots, then breathe clean air out of their leaves

19 DO PLANTS ON LAND PRODUCE MORE OXYGEN THAN OCEAN PLANTS?

A Plants in the ocean make more oxygen than plants on land

B Plants on land make more oxygen than all the plants in the ocean

C Plants on land and plants in the ocean make the same amount of oxygen

20 HOW MUCH WATER IS IN ALL THE OCEANS?

A The same amount as if you ran a tap for 1,200 years

B The same amount as a billion Olympic-sized swimming pools would hold

C About 1,260 million trillion litres

21 WHY DO FISH HAVE SCALES?

A   To help them to swim fast in the water

B   So that they look beautiful

C   To protect their bodies

22 HOW LONG DOES IT TAKE FOR A BABY SWAN TO GROW INTO A BIG SWAN?

A   Four weeks

B   Four months

C   Up to four years

23 WHY ARE GINGER CATS NORMALLY MALE?

A   Because male cats eat orange food, which turns their fur ginger

B   Because the gene that makes cats ginger is on the X chromosome

C   Because there are more male cats in the world overall, including more ginger cats

24 HOW MANY TYPES OF MEOW DOES A CAT HAVE?

A   More than 60, and each has a specific meaning

B   Only one, but they have lots of purrs

C   It depends on the breed of cat, because each breed has its own special meows

25 WHY DO CATS HISS?

A To pretend to be snakes

B Because they have seen a mouse

C Because they feel worried
or threatened

26 WHAT IS THE MOST POISONOUS FROG IN THE WORLD?

A The don't-eat-me-or-else frog

B The poison arrow frog

C The golden poison arrow frog

27 WHAT IS THE DEADLIEST ANIMAL IN THE WORLD?

A The mosquito

B The great white shark

C The crocodile

28 WHY DON'T SPIDERS GET STUCK ON THEIR WEBS?

A Because they have liquid on their feet that gets rid of stickiness

B Because they make sure to wash the sticky stuff off their feet

C Because they make two types of silk for their webs – sticky and not sticky – and try to only walk on the not-sticky bits

29 HOW ARE SPIDERS BORN?

A Out of a female spider

B Out of their webs

C Out of eggs

30 HOW DO SPIDERS SLEEP?

A   By hanging upside down in their webs like bats

B   By wrapping themselves up in their web like it's a silky sheet

C   They don't sleep like humans do – instead, they rest by not moving around

1 WHY ARE SLOTHS SO SLOW?

A Because they are super lazy and can't be bothered to move much

B Because they are greedy and always eat too much, so they find it hard to move

C Because they eat food that is low in energy, so they have to save their energy

2 WHICH ANIMALS ARE MOST CLOSELY RELATED TO SLOTHS?

A Walruses

B Koalas

C Anteaters and armadillos

3   HOW DOES A PIANO MAKE SOUND?

A   Pressing a piano key sends air through little pipes inside the piano that make noise

B   Pressing a piano key makes a hammer hit a string that vibrates

C   When you press a piano key, the warmth from your finger creates vibrations that make sound

4   WHY IS MILK WHITE?

A   Because it makes your bones stronger, and bones are white

B   Because the proteins in milk bunch together and make it look white

C   It is only white when it comes from white cows

5 WHAT ARE EGG YOLKS MADE OF?

A Yolker, a fatty substance a bit like curdled cheese

B Calcium and salt

C Protein, fat, lecithin and other things

6 WHY DO BEES STING?

A To defend themselves

B Because they are super mean and like to hurt other creatures

C To make their honey taste delicious

7 DO BEES HAVE KNEES?

A Sort of

B No

C Bumblebees have knees, but other bees do not

8 WHY IS THERE A QUEEN BEE?

A The bees need a queen to rule them

B To lay eggs for the hive

C To take care of all the female bees

9 WHERE DID APPLES FIRST COME FROM?

A South America

B Kazakhstan

C China

10 WHICH WAS CALLED ORANGE FIRST – THE FRUIT OR THE COLOUR?

A The fruit

B The colour

C The fruit and the colour were named at the same time

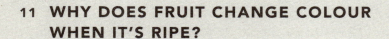

11 WHY DOES FRUIT CHANGE COLOUR WHEN IT'S RIPE?

A Because the fruit is actually dead

B Because it gets juicy, and the juice is what changes the colour

C To help it stay ripe, and to show animals and humans that it's ready to eat!

12 WHAT DO YOU CALL MORE THAN ONE BANANA?

A A bananarama

B A bunch

C A hand

13 CAN YOU EAT OTHER PARTS OF A BANANA PLANT BESIDES THE BANANAS?

A   Yes, lots of the banana plant is edible

B   No

C   In Australia, banana plants also grow kanga fruit, which you can eat

14 HOW LONG CAN SNAILS SLEEP FOR?

A   One month

B   72 weeks

C   Three years

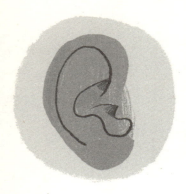

15 CAN SLUGS HEAR?

A Some species can, but others cannot

B No, because they don't have ears

C Yes, their antennae are ears

16 WHAT COLOUR IS BEETLE BLOOD?

A Red

B Clear, or tinged yellow or green

C Blue

17 HOW LONG WAS THE LONGEST WORM EVER FOUND?

A 10 metres

B 55 metres

C 206 metres

18 WHY IS HONEY SWEET?

A Because bees add sugar to it

B So that it tastes delicious to bees and humans

C Because it is made from plant nectar

19 WHY DO PLANTS NEED WATER?

A To make their cells strong, and to stay cool

B To make and transport their own food

C For all of the reasons listed above

20 WHAT IS THE LARGEST FLOWER IN THE WORLD?

A The titan flower

B The goliath flower

C The corpse flower

21 COULD A TREE GROW SO HIGH THAT IT REACHES SPACE?

A Yes, but none ever has because humans keep cutting them down!

B No, the tallest trees only grow to about 100 metres

C No, trees can't grow taller than 50 metres

22 WHAT IS THE OLDEST LIVING THING STILL ALIVE?

A A clonal tree called Pando

B An ancient sea turtle living in the Pacific Ocean

C A form of bacteria

23 WHAT IS THE BUTTER LANTERN FESTIVAL?

A A celebration where people put a big pile of butter into a lantern, then send it into the sky

B A celebration where people use lanterns to melt a lot of butter, then eat it on toast

C A Tibetan celebration where people use yak butter to fuel lanterns, then send them into the sky

24 ARE THERE MORE HUMANS OR MORE CHICKENS IN THE WORLD?

A Chickens

B Humans

C There are roughly the same number of each

25 WHY DO LADYBIRDS HAVE SPOTS ON THEIR BACKS?

A To show how old they are

B To make them look attractive so they find a mate

C To make them look yucky so they scare away predators

26 WHY DO SOME TREES LOSE THEIR LEAVES IN THE AUTUMN?

A So that they can grow prettier ones in spring

B So that they can save energy and survive the winter

C Because bees hibernate during winter and stop pollinating, so the trees don't need their leaves

27 HOW DO SNAILS STICK TO LEAVES WHEN THEY ARE UPSIDE DOWN?

A   By tying themselves on with a fancy ribbon

B   By piercing a hole in the leaf and attaching themselves to the other side

C   With sticky slime

28 WHY DO CHAMELEONS CHANGE COLOUR?

A   To reflect their moods, defend their territory and attract mates

B   To regulate their temperature

C   To communicate with other chameleons

29 HOW DO GECKOS CLEAN THEIR EYES IF THEY DON'T HAVE EYELIDS?

A They have little windscreen wipers to clean their eyeballs

B With a tissue or a flannel

C By licking them with their tongue

30 WHAT IS THE BIGGEST LIZARD TO EVER EXIST?

A The huge hairy scary gecko

B The Megalania

C The Komodo dragon

31 HOW DO KOMODO DRAGONS FIND FOOD?

A   They mostly order takeaway from nearby islands

B   They hunt for fish in the ocean

C   They eat meat by stalking animals that they smell with their forked tongues

1 IS THERE SUNKEN TREASURE IN THE OCEAN?

A No, pirates always hide their treasure on land in a spot marked "X"

B There used to be, but humans have found it all now using satellites and robots

C Yes, billions of pounds' worth

2 HOW DEEP IS THE DEEPEST PART OF THE OCEAN?

A 1,930 metres

B 10,930 metres

C 100,930 metres

3 WHAT IS THE BIGGEST ISLAND IN THE WORLD?

A Greenland

B Iceland

C Madagascar

4 HOW DO SPONGES SOAK UP WATER?

A By stretching their molecules

B Through their holes

C Through their fibres

5 WHY DO TREES HAVE BARK?

A To protect them like a hard skin

B So that animals can scratch their backs against them

C So that animals can climb up into the branches

6 WHY DO TREES' LEAVES GO ORANGE OR YELLOW IN THE AUTUMN?

A Because plants break down chlorophyll in autumn, and other chemicals are left behind

B Because the autumn sun turns them different colours

C Because all the autumn rain washes the green colour out

7 WHY DO PEOPLE DRINK WATER?

A To wash the insides of their bodies

B To keep their bodies working well

C So that the creatures in their tummies can have a nice swim

8 WHY DOES OUR SKIN GO WRINKLY IN THE BATH?

A So that we can hold on to things more easily

B To warn us that we have been sitting in there too long

C Because we are starting to transform into fish

9 WHY DO OUR EYES GO RED WHEN WE ARE TIRED?

A Because they get dry from being open for too long

B Because lots of blood needs to go to them to keep them open

C Because the more tired we are, the more allergic we are to things

10 WHICH IS TALLER – A BABY GIRAFFE OR A PERSON?

A A baby giraffe

B A person, but only if they're an adult

C A baby giraffe and an average seven-year-old person are the same size

11 WHICH ANIMAL HAS THE BIGGEST BABY?

A An elephant

B A giraffe

C A blue whale

12 DO BABY ELEPHANTS DRINK WITH THEIR TRUNKS?

A Yes, just like adult elephants do

B No, it takes about a year for an elephant to learn to use its trunk

C No, usually an adult elephant squirts water into a baby's mouth

13 DO ANY OTHER ANIMALS SUCK THEIR THUMBS?

A   No, only human babies

B   Yes, chimpanzees and other primates have been spotted sucking their thumbs

C   Newborn elephants suck their trunks

14 WHY DO ELEPHANTS HAVE LONG TRUNKS?

A   So that they can eat and drink as much as possible

B   So that they can sneeze loudly and scare other animals away

C   So that they snore loudly at night and no predators come near them

15 WHAT IS THE RAREST FLOWER IN THE WORLD?

A The Middleman's blue camellia

B The Middlemarch's yellow camellia

C The Middlemist's red camellia

16 HOW COLD IS PLUTO?

A 0°C

B −232°C

C It's too cold to measure!

17 WHAT WOULD HAPPEN IF YOU WENT INTO A BLACK HOLE?

A You'd get spaghettified

B You'd disintegrate into nothingness

C You'd enter a different universe on the other side

18 WHAT IS THE DIAMETER OF THE SUN?

A 621,000 miles (100,000 kilometres)

B About 870,000 miles (1.4 million kilometres)

C About 2 million miles (3.2 million kilometres)

19 WHERE IN THE WORLD WOULD YOU BE AS FAR AWAY AS POSSIBLE FROM ANY OTHER HUMANS?

A There are humans everywhere! So, if you want to be by yourself, the best thing to do is hide in your room

B Timbuktu in Mali

C Point Nemo in the southern Pacific Ocean

20 WHICH ANIMAL IS THERE THE MOST OF IN THE WORLD?

A Chickens

B Frogs

C Krill

21 WHICH OF THESE COUNTRIES HAS NO CAPITAL?

A Malawi

B Nauru

C Brazil

22 WHAT WAS THE FIRST FOOD THAT HUMANS MADE?

A Yoghurt

B Bread

C Cooked meat

23 WHY IS THE SKY BLUE?

A Because the Sun releases a blue gas that fills it

B Because there are lots of tiny blue insects floating in it

C Because the Earth's atmosphere scatters the Sun's light, and waves of blue light are scattered the most

24 HOW DOES RAIN GET INTO THE CLOUDS?

A Water in the air cools and comes together to make clouds, then freezes and melts, and drops on to your head as rain

B The Sun warms up ice crystals in the clouds, which melt and fall as rain

C We don't know! It must be magic . . .

25 WHY DO CLOUDS MOVE?

A They don't! The Earth moves, and it just looks as if the clouds are moving

B They're moved by the gravitational force of the Moon

C The wind carries them

26 WHO RULED FOR THE LONGEST PERIOD OF TIME?

A Queen Elizabeth II of the United Kingdom

B King Louis XIV of France

C Tutankhamun, pharaoh of ancient Egypt

27 WHAT WAS THE LONGEST WAR?

A The Hundred Years' War

B The Reconquista

C The Cold War

28 HOW DOES SAND GET MADE?

A From dust transported to beaches by the wind

B When bits of rock, skeletons, shells and even animal poo break down

C When people walk on rocky beaches and break the rocks down into sand

29 WHO WERE THE FIRST SURFERS?

A Polynesians

B Californians

C Australians

30 CAN A TORTOISE FEEL YOU SCRATCHING ITS SHELL?

A No, the shell protects the tortoise and it can't feel anything that touches it

B Yes, a tortoise's shell is very sensitive to touch

C Yes, but it will only feel like a light tickle, even if you scratch the tortoise pretty hard

1 WHICH ANIMAL HAS THE FASTEST HEARTBEAT, AND WHICH HAS THE SLOWEST?

A   A shrew has the fastest, and a blue whale the slowest

B   A human has the fastest, and a mouse the slowest

C   An ant has the fastest, and an elephant the slowest

2 HOW DO DOLPHINS SLEEP?

A   They lie down on the bottom of the ocean, and use a rock as a pillow

B   They rest their heads on floating pieces of wood on the ocean's surface

C   They sleep while swimming

3 WHAT IS THE FASTEST FISH IN THE WORLD?

A   A great white shark

B   A tuna

C   A sailfish

4 WHICH ANIMAL HAS THE LONGEST TAIL?

A   On land a giraffe, and in the sea a blue whale

B   On land an elephant, and in the sea a dolphin

C   On land a horse, and in the sea a manatee

5 HOW DID BONOBOS GET THEIR NAME?

A   From the noise they shout at night in the jungle

B   From a misspelling of Bolobo, a town on the Congo River, in Africa, where they live

C   From Miss Jane Bonobo, who discovered them

6   WHERE DO ORANGUTANS SLEEP?

A   In nests

B   On the jungle floor

C   In lovely beds with soft pillows

7   HOW LONG DO ORANGUTANS USUALLY LIVE?

A   20–30 years

B   30–40 years

C   55–65 years

8   WHICH DRAGON WAS THE FIRST TO COME ALONG?

A   The first dragon walked out of the mist in Skye, in Scotland, when time began

B   Dragon myths have been around for so long that it's not possible to find the first

C   The first dragon was born in China – its mother was a snake, and its father was an eagle

9   HOW BIG WAS A MEGALODON?

A   15–18 metres long

B   20–30 metres long

C   100–120 metres long

10   WHAT ARE TEETH MADE OF?

A   Bone and cartilage

B   Calcium

C   Pulp, dentin, enamel and cementum

11   WHAT IS THE LONGEST BONE IN THE HUMAN BODY?

A   The spine

B   The humerus

C   The femur

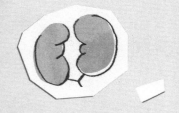

12 WHAT IS THE HEAVIEST ORGAN IN THE HUMAN BODY?

A The stomach

B The brain

C The skin

13 WHY DO WE HAVE LIPS?

A So that we have something to put lipstick and lip balm on

B So that we can make funny marks on windows

C To help us with eating, sucking and communicating

14 WHY IS THE SUN YELLOW?

A   Because it's so cheerful

B   It's not – it's white

C   It's only yellow sometimes because it keeps changing colour

15 ARE THERE STARS BEHIND THE SUN?

A   No, there is only sky and space

B   Yes, but we can't ever see them

C   Yes, and we can see them when the sky turns dark during a total solar eclipse

16 HOW LONG WOULD IT TAKE TO FLY TO THE MOON IN AN AEROPLANE?

A   450 years

B   One year and one day

C   Seventeen days

17 WHY DO STARS MOVE ACROSS THE SKY?

A   The wind blows them

B   They don't – it's the Earth that moves, not the stars

C   Angels in the sky push the stars along at night

18 WHY DO WOMBATS HAVE POUCHES?

A To carry their favourite snacks in

B To carry their babies in

C To keep their phones in

19 WHICH ANIMAL SLEEPS THE MOST?

A A sloth

B A giraffe

C A koala

20 IS A WOBBEGONG A REAL ANIMAL OR A MADE-UP ANIMAL?

A A what-a-gong? Made-up!

B It's made-up, but everyone has heard of it so it sort of exists

C Real! It's a type of shark

21 WHAT IS THE BIGGEST MARSUPIAL EVER?

A   A giant kangaroo

B   A massive koala

C   A big creature with two sticky-out teeth called a diprotodon

22 COULD YOU SEE IF YOU WERE INVISIBLE?

A   Of course you could!

B   No way!

C   It would depend on whether or not everything else was also invisible

23 HOW DO ECHOES WORK?

A Echo goblins repeat what you say when you speak into large, empty spaces

B The sound waves from your voice travel through the air and bounce off hard surfaces, then travel back to your ears!

C Echoes are just your imagination playing tricks on you

24 WHAT IS A SHADOW?

A Something attached to your body that you can never get rid of

B Something that forms when light hits an object it can't travel through

C Something caused by darkness coming out of objects

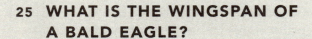

**25 WHAT IS THE WINGSPAN OF
A BALD EAGLE?**

A 2.1 metres

B 3.8 metres

C 7 metres

**26 HOW LONG DO VULTURES
USUALLY LIVE?**

A Around five years

B Up to 100 years

C Up to 47 years, depending on the species

27 WHY DOES GRAVITY PULL THINGS DOWN?

A It doesn't – if it did, we'd all be squished

B Because otherwise we'd float off into space

C It doesn't – it just feels like down, because gravity is a force of attraction

28 WHAT IS THE LONGEST SNAKE?

A A cobra

B A reticulated python

C An anaconda

29 HOW MUCH OF A SNAKE IS ITS TAIL?

A   A snake is *all* tail and no body

B   Snakes don't have tails

C   It depends on the species

30 CAN SNAKES BLINK?

A   Yes, they blink often, just like humans do

B   Yes, they blink once an hour to clean their eyes

C   No

31 WHERE IS THE OLDEST ROCK?

A At Uluru, in Australia

B In the Grand Canyon, in the United States of America

C In the Acasta gneisses, in Canada

1   WHAT ARE PROFESSIONAL BADMINTON SHUTTLECOCKS MADE FROM?

A   Dried leaves

B   Fried potatoes

C   Goose feathers

2   WHO WAS THE FIRST MODERN OLYMPIC GAMES MEDALLIST?

A   A swimmer who won freestyle

B   A triple-jump athlete

C   A 100-metre runner

3   WHY IS THE SPORT CRICKET CALLED CRICKET?

A   Because cricket bats look like cricket insects

B   It comes from the Middle Dutch word for a stick

C   Because of the sound the ball makes as it hits the bat

**4   WHAT IS THE BIGGEST CRAB
     IN THE WORLD?**

A   The gigantic monster crab

B   The massive long-legs crab

C   The Japanese spider crab

5   DO COCONUT CRABS EAT COCONUTS?

A   Yes, they eat them if they can find them

B   No, they can't crack coconuts open

C   Yes, coconuts are the only things they eat

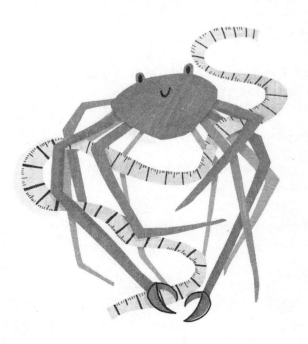

6 HOW MANY TEETH DOES A JAGUAR HAVE?

A 15

B 120

C 30

7 HOW DO SHARKS CLEAN THEIR TEETH?

A They don't need to

B They have special toothbrushes made from algae

C The seawater cleans their teeth for them

8 HOW MANY TEETH DOES A SHARK HAVE?

A 1,000

B Between 50 and 300, depending on what kind of shark it is

C All adult species (apart from the nurse shark) have 86

9 WHY DO WE HAVE EYEBROWS?

A To protect the area of skin underneath

B To protect our eyes and help us express ourselves

C To make us look more beautiful

10 WHY DO PEOPLE GET FRECKLES?

A From being in the sun

B From not getting enough daylight

C From eating spotty bananas

11 WHY DO WE GET BRUISES WHEN WE FALL OVER?

A Because some of our veins burst

B Because all the cells that rush over to help with the pain are blue

C So that we can show our friends how brave we have been

12 HOW MUCH OF A WATERMELON IS WATER?

A 92 per cent

B 85 per cent

C 75 per cent

13 IS ICE CREAM A SOLID OR A LIQUID?

A A solid

B A liquid

C A solid, a liquid *and* a gas!

14 WHAT YEAR WAS ICE CREAM INVENTED?

A Around 1515, in Renaissance Italy

B 1050 in India, because it got very hot

C We don't know!

15 HOW MANY TIMES A SECOND DOES A WOODPECKER PECK?

A Two

B 20

C 200

16 HOW MUCH NECTAR DO HUMMINGBIRDS DRINK?

A Half their body weight each day

B More than their own body weight each day

C Five times their own body weight each day

17 ARE THERE ANY PARROTS THAT CAN'T FLY?

A   Yes, the kākāpō

B   No

C   Yes, there are three – the macaw, the soft-beaked pippin and the kākāpō

18 WHY DO AYE-AYES HAVE LONG FINGERS?

A   To pick their noses

B   To scoop bugs out of hiding places to eat

C   To wave hello to their friends

19 WHY DO PEOPLE SHED TEARS WHEN THEY ARE HAPPY OR SAD?

A Tears allow people to express their emotions without words

B Nobody has figured out exactly why people cry

C Most people can shed tears whenever they want to, even if they are not happy or sad

20 WHY DO PEOPLE SNORE?

A It's how some people's bodies react to nightmares

B Because they have colds and their noses are blocked

C Because their breath makes their tongues, mouths, throats or airways vibrate

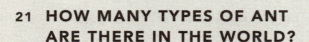

21 HOW MANY TYPES OF ANT ARE THERE IN THE WORLD?

A Approximately 1,200

B About 3 million

C More than 12,000

22 WHAT ARE A FLY'S WINGS MADE OF?

A Cuticle

B Really tiny bones

C Silken threads which the fly spins out of its mouth and makes into wings at night

23 HOW FAST CAN HONEYBEES FLY?

A Up to 40 miles (64 kilometres) per hour –
about the speed of a gazelle

B Up to 30 miles (48 kilometres) per hour –
about the speed of a cat

C Up to 20 miles (32 kilometres) per hour –
about the speed of a squirrel

**24 WHAT IS THE TALLEST MOUNTAIN IN
THE WORLD, FROM BASE TO SUMMIT?**

A Mount Everest/Chomolungma in the Himalaya

B Mount Kilimanjaro in Tanzania

C Mauna Kea in Hawai'i

25 WHAT IS THE WORLD'S OLDEST ACTIVE VOLCANO?

A Ben Nevis in Scotland

B Hunga Tonga–Hunga Ha'apai in Tonga

C Mount Etna in Italy

26 WHAT IS THE LONGEST RIVER IN THE WORLD?

A The Zambezi River

B The River Thames

C Either the Nile or the Amazon

27 WHY DO OCTOPUSES SHOOT OUT INK?

A   To escape from and scare away predators

B   Because they are very creative and like making patterns

C   To attack

28 HOW MANY EYES DOES AN OCTOPUS HAVE?

A   One

B   Two

C   Eight

29 HOW MANY HEARTS DOES AN OCTOPUS HAVE?

A One

B Two

C Three

30 HOW DOES A SEAHORSE SWIM?

A By flapping its wings

B By swishing its tail

C Using a small fin on its back

31 WHY DO SQUIDS AND OCTOPUSES HAVE BEAKS LIKE PARROTS?

A To help them to kill then chop up sea creatures for their food

B So that they can squawk like a parrot

C So that they can peck things like parrots do

1 WHY DO BURPS AND FARTS SOUND SO DIFFERENT?

A Because they come from different places in your body, so they're created in different ways

B Actually, each person's burps and farts sound the same – it is just that farts are further from our ears, so they sound different!

C So that others know whether to run away or not – if someone farts, you need to run!

2 WHAT HAPPENS TO WEE AND POO WHEN WE FLUSH THE TOILET?

A They disappear like magic

B They go into a giant bucket, then get turned into electricity

C They go down pipes to a factory where they get cleaned with other wee and poo, then they're sent out into a river or the sea

3 WHAT DOES "CHECKMATE" MEAN IN CHESS?

A That's it, mate – game over!

B You'd better check your move, my friend!

C The king is dead!

4 WHO INVENTED SCRABBLE?

A Mr Querty

B Mr A. B. Letters

C Mr Alfred Mosher Butts

5   WHAT IS THE HIGHEST SCORE YOU CAN GET IN ONE SCRABBLE WORD?

A   392 with CAZIQUES

B   1,782 with OXYPHENBUTAZONE

C   There is no limit to the highest score you can get

6   WHERE WAS THE GAME SNAKES AND LADDERS INVENTED?

A   India

B   Indonesia

C   Iceland

7   WHERE WAS THE FIRST CARPET MADE?

A   Armenia

B   Greece

C   Peru

8 WHERE WAS YOGA INVENTED?

A Bhutan

B Bali

C India

9 WHO WROTE THE VERY FIRST WRITING?

A The Sumerians

B The ancient Egyptians

C Some poets in a café in Paris

10 WHERE WAS PAPER INVENTED?

A China

B England

C Indonesia

11 WHAT CAUSES A STITCH WHEN YOU RUN?

A Your heart

B We don't know

C Being short of breath

12 WHICH ANIMAL HAS THE LOUDEST CALL?

A A gorilla

B A howler monkey

C A blue whale

13 WHY DO ALL MAMMALS HAVE HAIR OR FUR?

A So that they have something to brush or lick clean in the morning

B To provide a layer of insulation to keep them warm

C To make them more attractive to other mammals

14 HOW DO BOGEYS FORM IN YOUR NOSE?

A Little goblins come out at night and put them in there

B They are dried-up bits of mucus, dirt and bacteria

C The body creates them as a protective barrier

15 WHY DO YOUR CHEEKS GO RED?

A Because you have eaten too much red food, like ketchup or strawberries

B As a sign that you are in distress and possibly angry

C To relax the muscles in your face in times of stress, anxiety or heat

16 WHY DO HUMANS HAVE TOENAILS?

A So that we have nails to paint

B Because we used to need them before we wore shoes

C To protect the tops of our toes

17 CAN CATS SEE THE SAME THINGS AS HUMANS CAN?

A   No, cats have better vision in the dark but can't see colours as well as we do

B   No, and they can see exactly the same whether it's day or night

C   Yes, cats can see the same things as us

18 WHY DO SOME CATS HATE WATER?

A   Because they're scared of it

B   Because it doesn't feel nice on their fur

C   Because they can't swim

19 WHY DON'T CATS HAVE EYELASHES?

A Most cats do!

B Because they have so much fur round their eyes they don't need any

C Because it would make them look too scary to mice, so they have evolved not to have them

20 WHY DO LYNXES HAVE TUFTS OF FUR ON THE TOPS OF THEIR EARS?

A Probably to help them hear better

B Probably to help keep their ears warm

C Probably to make them look attractive to other lynxes

21 WHAT IS THE DIFFERENCE BETWEEN A JAGUAR AND A LEOPARD?

A   Jaguars are about 20 per cent larger, but otherwise they are the same

B   They have different jaws, heads and tails, and live on different continents

C   The only difference is their fur pattern

22 DO SEAGULLS WEE?

A   No

B   Yes

C   Yes, but it's white

23 WHERE DO MOST BIRDS SLEEP AT NIGHT?

A   High up in the trees

B   In little burrows underground

C   In nests

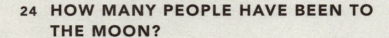

24 HOW MANY PEOPLE HAVE BEEN TO THE MOON?

A Only two have walked on it, but lots have been close to it

B No one has ever been to the Moon

C 24 have flown to the Moon, but only twelve have landed on it

25 WHY DO STARS ONLY COME OUT AT NIGHT?

A They are out during the day, too, but we can't see them because of the sunlight

B Because they are sleeping during the day

C Because they need the light of the Moon to make them twinkle

26 WHY DO CLOCKS SPIN CLOCKWISE?

A   Because we read from left to right, so it makes sense that clocks should spin the same way

B   Because sundials – the first clocks – moved clockwise

C   Because the inventor of clocks decided that's the way they should spin

27 HOW MANY VOLTS OF ELECTRICITY CAN A LEMON PRODUCE?

A   0.07 volts

B   0.7 volts

C   7 volts

28 HOW HIGH CAN A FLYING FISH FLY?

A Up to 200 metres

B Up to 20 metres

C Up to 2 metres

29 WHY DO SEA TURTLES HIDE IN THEIR SHELLS?

A To keep them safe from creatures that might try to eat them

B Because they're sleepy

C They don't hide in their shells

30 WHY ARE DOLPHINS SO SOFT?

A Because they use a lot of moisturizer

B Because the sea water is really good for their skin

C Because their outer layer of skin cells is replaced every few hours

1 WHY DO LIONS HAVE FUR ON THE ENDS OF THEIR TAILS?

A   To keep their tails warm

B   To communicate and help to show where they are

C   So that they can stroke their faces with their fluffy tails

2 WHY DO MALE LIONS HAVE MANES?

A   To show how strong they are and to protect their necks

B   To keep their necks warm at night

C   So that they can make a nice pillow for their babies to sleep on

3 WHAT IS THE LOUDEST ANIMAL ALIVE TODAY?

A The lion

B The whale shark

C The tiger pistol shrimp

4 WHICH PREDATORY CAT IS THE BIGGEST?

A The snow leopard

B The jaguar

C The Siberian tiger

5 WHAT IS THE BIGGEST NUMBER?

A A quadrillion

B A billion

C A googolplex

6 WHAT IS THE OFFICIAL CURRENCY OF CHINA?

A The renminbi

B The yuan

C The Chinese dollar

7 IN NORSE MYTHOLOGY, WHAT IS THE NAME OF THE GODDESS FREYA'S BROTHER?

A Baldr

B Thor

C Freyr

8 WHERE IS THE WORLD'S BIGGEST WATERFALL?

A Iguazu Falls in Brazil, Argentina and Paraguay

B The Denmark Strait, a waterfall below the Atlantic Ocean

C Niagara Falls, in the United States of America and Canada

9 WHERE IS THE LONGEST BEACH IN THE WORLD?

A Along the coast of Chile

B In Western Australia

C In Brazil

10 HOW DO OYSTERS MAKE PEARLS?

A Out of annoying things like worms that enter their shells – oysters cover them in a special substance called nacre, and they become pearls!

B By collecting shiny shells and smashing them, then rolling them into balls

C No one knows, because oysters keep their pearl recipe a secret – and that's why pearls are so expensive!

11 WHAT IS THE LIGHTEST ELEMENT IN THE UNIVERSE?

A Air

B Water

C Hydrogen

12 WHY IS THERE NO GRAVITY IN SPACE?

A There *is* gravity in space

B Because the air molecules are too far apart in space

C Because there are no apple trees to sit under, so there isn't much point in having gravity, as no apples can fall from trees

13 WHAT ARE STARS MADE OF?

A Glitter and magic

B Sparkle dust

C Very hot gases

14 WHAT IS THE TALLEST ROCKET TO HAVE FLOWN INTO SPACE?

A The *Mars XII*

B The *Apollo XIII*

C The *Saturn V*

15 WHERE IS THE BIGGEST POPCORN MACHINE IN THE WORLD?

A In a cinema in Hollywood, in the United States of America

B At a theme park in Phuket, in Thailand

C In the inventor of popcorn's back garden

16 HOW IS BUTTER MADE?

A By mixing sugar and yoghurt together

B By churning cream taken out of fresh milk

C By combining honey and sunshine

17 HOW IS SPARKLING WATER MADE FIZZY?

A By stirring it up really fast

B By adding carbon dioxide

C By blowing bubbles into it with a giant straw machine

18 WHAT DOES THE WORD PACIFIC MEAN IN PACIFIC OCEAN?

A Peaceful

B Huge

C Piece, because it's just one piece of all the oceans across Earth

19 CAN WHALES SING?

A No, they are pretty much silent creatures

B Yes, they sing long, deep songs that can travel for miles through the oceans

C Some do, and some don't! Just like humans, some love singing, while others get embarrassed or shy

20 CAN YOU HEAR ANYTHING AT THE BOTTOM OF THE OCEAN?

A   No, it's spookily silent because it's so deep

B   Yes, you can hear earthquakes, whale song and other noises

C   Yes, but the only thing you can hear down there is the sound of mermaids swishing their tails

21 HOW MANY BONES DO SHARKS HAVE IN THEIR BODIES?

A   Zero

B   108

C   355

22 WHAT ANIMAL LIVES THE LONGEST?

A A human

B A whale

C A clam

23 WHAT IS THE SMALLEST OWL IN THE WORLD?

A The teeny-tiny cute little owl

B The elf owl

C The polka-dot owl

24 DO ANY OWLS COME OUT DURING THE DAY?

A   No, owls are nocturnal, which means they're always out at night

B   Some do, such as the long-legged burrowing owl

C   Yes, most do, but we can't see them because they're invisible by day – magic!

25 WHY DOES A TRACTOR HAVE BIG WHEELS AND SMALL WHEELS?

A   Because it's important for the driver to be sitting up high, so that they can see the field they are ploughing

B   Because having larger wheels at the back prevents it from getting stuck in the mud

C   Because having smaller wheels at the front makes it possible to steer the tractor

26 WHAT IS THE FASTEST TRAIN IN THE WORLD?

A   The Shanghai Maglev in China

B   The TGV in France

C   The Shinkansen (known in English as bullet trains) in Japan

27 HOW DO WHALES SLEEP?

A   By lying down on the ocean floor

B   By hanging vertically or horizontally, or by swimming slowly next to another whale

C   They don't sleep, because they don't need to

28 HOW MANY BONES ARE IN A WHALE'S NECK?

A One long, bendy one

B Seven

C 23

29 WHAT IS THE WORLD'S SMALLEST BAT?

A The little brown bat

B The bumblebee bat

C The Honduran white bat

30 WHY DO HUMANS NEED BONES?

A   So that we have something to put clothes on to keep warm

B   To support and protect our bodies, and to keep our blood, hearts and muscles healthy

C   So that we can get together as skeletons for Halloween

31 WHY DO WE CARVE FACES ON PUMPKINS FOR HALLOWEEN?

A   To light the way for ghosts and witches

B   To scare away ghosts

C   Just for fun

1 WHAT DOES DIWALI MEAN?

A "Row of lights" in Sanskrit

B "Happy New Year" in Sanskrit

C "Time for fireworks" in Sanskrit

2 WHY DO CAMELS SPIT?

A To scare or surprise other creatures bothering them

B Because they've drunk too much water

C Because they're feeling really sick

3 WHAT IS THE LONGEST A DANCE PARTY HAS EVER LASTED IN THE WORLD?

A 230 hours

B 56 hours

C Four hours

4 HOW DO YOU MAKE GLASS?

A By catching clouds and freezing them

B By melting sand (or soda ash, or limestone) into a liquid, then letting it cool

C We don't – it occurs naturally in the ocean near Australia, and we dig it up

5 WHY IS BLUE CHEESE STINKY?

A Because the milk used to make it comes from a special kind of blue cow that is particularly stinky

B It's not – only children think it is stinky, because their noses are very sensitive

C Because it is full of mould

6 ON AVERAGE, HOW MUCH CHEESE DOES A PERSON IN THE UNITED KINGDOM EAT IN ONE YEAR?

A 1 kilogram – about the same weight as a pineapple

B 5 kilograms – about the same weight as a male cat

C Over 10 kilograms – about the same weight as a medium-sized dog

7 WHAT IS THE GERMAN BLUE RAM?

A A blue sheep

B A type of cheese

C A very colourful fish

8 WHY DID THE DINOSAURS BECOME EXTINCT WHEN AN ASTEROID HIT THE EARTH?

A Because the asteroid made a crater that covered the Earth, and the dinosaurs fell into it

B Because it changed the climate on Earth, so dinosaurs could no longer survive

C Because the dinosaurs didn't want to see any more asteroids, so they left for another planet

9 WHICH ANIMAL HAD EIGHT HEARTS?

A The prehistoric cockroach

B The *barosaurus*

C The hagfish

10 HOW LONG DO BLOBFISH LIVE FOR?

A One year

B Ten years

C 100 years

11 WHICH ANIMAL HAS THE MOST STRIPES?

A   A tiger

B   A zebra

C   A chipmunk

12 HOW DO GIRAFFES COMMUNICATE WITH EACH OTHER IF THEY CAN'T TALK?

A   By using telepathy

B   By stamping their feet and sending vibrations through the ground to one another

C   With their eyes, with touch, and with sounds including hums, grunts and moans that are too low for us to hear

13 WHICH ANIMAL HAS THE BIGGEST BRAIN?

A A human

B An elephant

C A sperm whale

14 WHY IS HIPPO SWEAT PINK?

A Because hippos eat a lot of strawberries

B Because it contains pink pigments which protect the hippo's skin

C Because it reacts with pink flowers that live in the water where hippos live

15 WHICH INSECT HAS THE BIGGEST BRAIN?

A An ant

B A ladybird

C A giant Japanese hornet

16 HOW LONG IS THE BIGGEST FLY?

A 7 centimetres

B 15 centimetres

C 35 centimetres

17 HOW DO SPIDERS STICK TO WALLS?

A Using little sticky pads on their feet

B Using tiny hairs on their feet

C By licking their feet and coating them with their sticky spit

18 WHY DO SNAILS COME OUT IN THE RAIN?

A   Because they usually mate in wet weather

B   Because they love to wash and shower in the rain

C   To keep their skin moist and avoid drying out

19 HOW LONG IS THE BIGGEST STICK INSECT?

A   35 centimetres

B   53 centimetres

C   89 centimetres

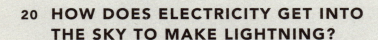

20 HOW DOES ELECTRICITY GET INTO THE SKY TO MAKE LIGHTNING?

A It shoots up out of televisions and into the sky

B During a storm, clouds become more negatively charged than the ground, and lightning balances this

C Energy from earthquakes rises and makes lightning

21 HOW DO SOLAR PANELS WORK?

A By collecting sunlight and turning it into electricity

B By powering a motor that turns, then turning the energy from this into electricity

C By using sunlight to recharge all the used batteries they are made of

22 WHY DO MAGNETS REPEL?

A They produce a magnetic field around them which, when two similar poles come together, pushes them apart

B To maintain balance in the universe

C Magnetic force is like the opposite of gravity, so it pushes things apart instead of pulling them together

23 HOW HEAVY IS THE HEAVIEST WOLF?

A 70 kilograms – about the same as a washing machine

B 181 kilograms – about the same as the heart of a blue whale

C 40 kilograms – about the same as an average loo

24 WHAT IS THE LATIN NAME FOR A RED FOX?

A *Vulpes lagopus*

B *Rufus vulpes*

C *Vulpes vulpes*

25 WHAT MAKES THE EYESIGHT OF NOCTURNAL ANIMALS SO GOOD AT NIGHT?

A They usually have bigger eyes with a layer like a mirror

B They have special eye cells that can sense very weak light

C Both of the above

26 ARE ANIMALS TICKLISH?

A No

B Yes, a number are

C Yes, but only humans and monkeys

27 WHY DO DIAMONDS SHINE?

A Because, in jewellery, they are cut cleverly to give them lots of surfaces to reflect light and make them shine

B Because they are full of sunlight, which shines out of them

C Because they contain a gas that sparkles inside when you shine a light on them

28 HOW IS CEMENT MADE?

A By mixing powder with water to make a paste

B By knocking down houses and grinding up their walls

C By crushing materials like limestone and clay, then mixing them together and heating them

29 WHAT IS THE TALLEST HOUSE IN THE WORLD?

A The White House in Washington, DC, in the United States of America

B Buckingham Palace in London, in the United Kingdom

C Falcon Nest in Prescott, Arizona, in the United States of America

**30 HOW MANY FLOORS DOES
A SKYSCRAPER HAVE?**

A   More than 100

B   More than 40

C   More than 255

1 CAN PENGUINS DRINK SEAWATER?

A No, they can only drink fresh water, so they love to drink rain

B Yes, they drink it all the time

C Penguins don't need to drink water because they get it from eating wet fish

2 ARE THERE ANY INSECTS IN ANTARCTICA?

A Yes, plenty – they live on the penguins

B Not a single one

C Just one species

3 WHAT ARE PENGUINS' BEAKS MADE OF?

A Keratin

B Bone

C Crab shells

4 WHY DO PENGUINS HAVE YELLOW BEAKS?

A Because it helps them to decide on a mate – they'll choose a penguin with a similar beak!

B Because they are bright and glow in the dark, which helps the penguins find one another at night

C So that they can see one another when swimming in the ocean

5   WHY DON'T POLAR BEARS SLIP ON THE ICE AND SNOW?

A   Because they are so heavy

B   They actually do slip – quite a lot!

C   Because they have pads on their feet that are covered in little bumps

6   HOW DO ICICLES FORM?

A   When it rains on cold days

B   When snowflakes get caught on each other and melt together

C   When ice melted by the Sun refreezes as it drips down

7 WHY DO HYENAS LAUGH?

A Because they are good at telling jokes

B Because they are frustrated, in conflict or hunting

C Because they are hurt

8 WHY DO ELEPHANTS HAVE BIG EARS?

A Because they're fun to wiggle

B To help them to cool down

C So that they can play peek-a-boo with baby elephants

9 WHAT IS THE DIFFERENCE BETWEEN AN ALLIGATOR AND A CROCODILE?

A Crocodiles have feathers at birth, but alligators don't

B You can see an alligator later, but you can see a crocodile in a while

C They have different snout shapes, teeth, habitats and behaviour

10 WHY IS IT SO DIFFICULT TO FIND A FOUR-LEAF CLOVER?

A It's not – the idea that it is hard is a myth

B Because cows love to eat them, so they're usually gobbled up first

C Because they're very rare – only one clover in 10,000 has four leaves

11 HOW LONG DO MUSHROOMS LIVE?

A A few weeks

B Up to two years

C Up to one month

12 WHAT IS THE MOST DANGEROUS PLANT IN THE WORLD?

A The castor oil plant

B Deadly nightshade

C The Whomping Willow tree

13 WHO INVENTED CHOCOLATE?

A Sweet-shop owners in Switzerland

B The Olmecs, an ancient civilization who lived in modern-day Central America

C A lady from Cadbury, in England

14 WHAT IS THE RECORD FOR THE WORLD'S FASTEST ROLLERCOASTER?

A   80 miles (129 kilometres) per hour

B   149 miles (240 kilometres) per hour

C   212 miles (341 kilometres) per hour

15 WHO WAS THE FIRST PERSON TO BUILD A ROBOT?

A   English scientist Charles Darwin

B   American engineer George Devol

C   German-born scientist Albert Einstein

16 WHO INVENTED SHOES?

A   People who lived in modern-day South America over 3,000 years ago

B   We don't know!

C   An inventor known as Cobblerius back in the year 12 BCE

17 WHY DO WE YAWN?

A Because seeing someone else do it makes us want to yawn, too

B To make us more alert when we're under-stimulated

C Both of the above

18 WHY DO PEOPLE FART?

A Because they need to go to the loo

B Because it makes people laugh

C To get rid of gases that build up from digesting food and swallowing air

19 WHERE ARE RED BLOOD CELLS MADE?

A In the heart

B In the bone marrow

C In the brain

20 HOW MANY LEGS DOES A ROBIN HAVE?

A Two

B Three

C Six

21 WHY DO WE DECORATE CHRISTMAS TREES?

A So that Father Christmas will see our houses shining

B So that kids have somewhere to hang all the decorations they've made at school

C Because fir trees have been used to celebrate winter festivals for thousands of years

22 HOW ARE ROBINS RELATED TO CHRISTMAS?

A Their red breasts look like Father Christmas's jacket

B Their red breasts look like postal workers' jackets

C Their red breasts look like Christmas baubles

23 HOW LONG DOES IT TAKE TO GROW A CHRISTMAS TREE?

A Up to fifteen years

B Between six and ten years

C Up to two years

24 WHERE DOES THE IDEA OF FATHER CHRISTMAS COME FROM?

A From the three wise men who gave baby Jesus presents

B From Saint Nicholas

C From a very tall elf

25 WHO INVENTED CHRISTMAS CRACKERS?

A Mr and Mrs Cracker

B Charles Dickens

C An English sweet maker

26 ARE ALL SNOWFLAKES DIFFERENT SHAPES?

A No, they all look the same

B It's unlikely you'll ever see two snowflakes that are the same shape

C It depends where you are, because each country has its own special shape of snowflake

27 HOW DO HELICOPTERS FLY?

A By balancing on the wind

B By spinning the blades on top so fast that a tornado effect is created beneath the helicopter and lifts it up

C By spinning the blades on top so fast that the air moves faster over the top of the helicopter than under it, and this creates lift

28 WHERE DOES ELECTRICITY COME FROM?

A   Energy sources, such as wind or fossil fuels or the Sun

B   It's magic!

C   Our minds – when we believe in electricity, it works

29 HOW DO MICROWAVE OVENS COOK THINGS?

A   By blasting the food with invisible lasers

B   By heating up like a super-charged oven

C   By heating the water molecules in food

30 WHY IS A YEAR 365 DAYS LONG?

A Because that's about how long it takes for the Moon to complete a full journey round the Earth

B No one really knows – someone made a 365-day calendar a long time ago, and it's just stayed that way!

C Because that's about how long it takes for the Earth to complete a full journey round the Sun

31 HOW MANY WORDS ARE THERE IN THE ENGLISH DICTIONARY?

A 89,935

B 171,476

C More than a million, but we don't know for sure!

ANSWERS

1 JANUARY

A Giant dragon bamboo can grow to 46 metres tall and 37 centimetres wide – that's about the same height as the Statue of Liberty in New York, in the United States of America!

2 JANUARY

B Approximately 385,000 babies are born in the world every day! That's about 267 babies born every minute, and more than 140 million in a year.

3 JANUARY

C According to Buzz Aldrin, one of the two Apollo 11 astronauts who walked on the Moon in 1969, it smelled like gunpowder! Moon rocks that have been brought back to Earth don't have a smell, however, so it seems you have to go to the Moon to find out exactly how it smells. Elsewhere in our solar system, the planet Uranus has a lot of hydrogen sulphide in its atmosphere, so we think it might smell like rotten eggs!

4 JANUARY

C The Moon is grey. It just looks yellow and shiny a lot of the time because its surface reflects light from the Sun. Up close it looks grey, and if you picked up a rock from the Moon it would be grey. And, although we sometimes say "once in a blue moon", the moon is never blue!

5 JANUARY

A If the Earth were a tennis ball, the Moon would be a marble. The Moon has a radius of about 1,080 miles (1,740 kilometres), making it more than three times smaller than Earth.

6 JANUARY

A There are 7 quintillion 500 quadrillion grains of sand on Earth. To figure this out, researchers in Hawai'i first worked out the average size of a grain of sand, then how many grains there were in a teaspoon, then multiplied that by all the beaches and deserts on Earth!

7 JANUARY

C You need sunlight and raindrops to make a rainbow, and at the moment we don't know of any planet besides Earth that has either liquid water on its surface or enough water in its atmosphere to create rain. So, for now, our beautiful planet is the only one we know of where you get rainbows. How lucky we are!

8 JANUARY

C You can't dig through the Earth, but if you could, England's antipode – or opposite point – would be in the Pacific Ocean, 500 miles (800 kilometres) south of Rēkohu/Chatham Island. You'd need to start digging somewhere off the east coast of the United States of America, in the Atlantic Ocean, to end up in or near Australia!

9 JANUARY

C Kangaroos are herbivores most of the time, which means they eat plants. They mainly eat grass, leaves, ferns and moss, but will sometimes eat insects, too. In the past, there were once giant meat-eating kangaroos that had fangs like wolves!

10 JANUARY

A Chlorine is put in pools to kill germs. In water, it makes something called hypochlorous acid, which kills off nasty bacteria, such as salmonella and *E. coli*, which can cause vomiting and diarrhea.

11 JANUARY

C   Cows only have one stomach, but it is made of four parts: the rumen, the reticulum, the omasum and the abomasum.

12 JANUARY

A   The real problem isn't cows farting – it's humans. When we farm lots of cows for meat and dairy, and feed them unhealthy diets such as soya beans, they make farts and burps that are full of a greenhouse gas called methane. We need some greenhouse gases – however, if there is too much, the planet gets *too* warm, and that's a problem. Humans do all kinds of things that produce greenhouse gases, but worst of all is burning fossil fuels to power machines like cars. The greenhouse gases that humans produce is what has caused Earth's climate to change. This is bad for the environment because it makes it hard for everything – humans and plants and animals alike – to carry on living. The good news is, we know it's humans producing the harmful greenhouse gases, and we also know we need to stop. So, when it comes to farming cows, we need to feed them on plants and grass, and also make sure we eat less meat and dairy, and then there won't be so many cows – and their farts won't be a problem any more!

13 JANUARY

C Earth is in a solar system that formed out of a huge cloud of gas and dust that collapsed and started to spin around 4.6 billion years ago. As this happened, bits of the spinning cloud of gas and dust formed into the Sun in the middle, and other bits formed into the planets around it – including Earth – which kept spinning.

14 JANUARY

A You could fit 1.3 million Earths inside the Sun.

15 JANUARY

A We move with the Earth, as does everything around us – the trees, the oceans, the buildings, the people, the creatures, the atmosphere – and that is why we can't feel it. The Earth moves very slowly, but if it jerked about we might be able to feel it moving.

16 JANUARY

C Different parts of the Sun are different temperatures, but the core is 15 million degrees Celsius. It gets cooler as you get closer to the surface, where it is 5,500 degrees Celsius.

Every 1.5 millionths of a second, the Sun releases more energy than all the humans on Earth use in a whole year!

17 JANUARY

A   The Inaccessible Island rail is a teeny bird that lives on (you guessed it!) Inaccessible Island in Tristan da Cunha, a group of volcanic islands in the Atlantic Ocean. This little brown bird has a black beak and feet, and the adults have red eyes! On the island it calls home, it doesn't have any predators, so it's OK that it can't fly.

18 JANUARY

C   Feathers help birds to fly – but even birds that don't fly, such as kiwi and ostrich, have feathers. They're also super handy for showing off to other birds, providing camouflage so as not to be spotted by predators, and keeping warm and dry!

19 JANUARY

C   Flamingos are pink because of their food! They eat algae and shrimps, which are full of natural pink colours called pigments. As flamingos eat their food, they digest these pigments, turning their feathers pink.

20 JANUARY

A Over 65,000 years ago, a bird nicknamed the demon duck of doom lived across Australia. Its scientific name is *Genyornis newtoni*, and it's also known as the thunder bird or mihirung paringmal (meaning "giant bird" in Tjapwuring, the language of the Djab Wurrung people of Australia). It couldn't fly, was two metres tall, weighed 200 kilograms, laid eggs the size of watermelons and had a huge beak. It's possible this massive duck went extinct because humans kept eating its enormous eggs! I wonder how big an omelette you could make with a watermelon-sized egg?

21 JANUARY

A A cassowary is a huge flightless bird in Australia and Papua New Guinea, and it makes a deep growling sound.

22 JANUARY

A Russia is the biggest country in the world by area. Covering 6,601,668 square miles (17,098,242 square kilometres), it makes up 11 per cent of the entire world's landmass!

23 JANUARY

B Most people in ancient Egypt were farmers, but they also did other jobs and liked to have fun, too. They lived in houses made of mud bricks along the Nile, which flooded every year, making the soil really fertile so lots of lovely things like wheat, barley, lettuce, flax and papyrus could grow. Then, the Egyptians worked out how to move river water to fields and grow fruit, olives and beans. They also liked swimming, canoeing, board games, music and dancing. And they also built the pyramids, of course!

24 JANUARY

A Titanosaurs were a group of long-necked sauropods that included the *Patagotitan* and the *Argentinosaurus*. Experts can't decide which was the bigger of the two!

25 JANUARY

C The *Nyasasaurus* is the earliest known dinosaur. It lived 243 million years ago in modern-day Tanzania.

26 JANUARY

B   We think dinosaurs became extinct because an asteroid hit the Earth.

27 JANUARY

B   Most dinosaur fossils have been found in Asia, followed by North America, then Europe. Only a few have been found in Antarctica and in Australasia.

28 JANUARY

C   Mercury is the smallest planet in our solar system. It's also the closest to the Sun.

29 JANUARY

A   Mars has a dense core of iron, nickel and sulphur. Outside that is a rocky mantle, and on top a crust of iron, magnesium, aluminium, calcium and potassium.

30 JANUARY

A   The closest star to Earth is, of course, the Sun! The next closest is Alpha Centauri.

31 JANUARY

C   The water droplets that make up clouds are so tiny, they're not affected by gravity. The average water droplet in a cloud is the size of a piece of dust. Just as dust can float in the air for a long time, water can float inside clouds.

1 FEBRUARY

B   It's like caterpillar soup inside a chrysalis! First, the caterpillar digests itself – so, if you were to cut a chrysalis open at the right time, liquid would ooze out. Inside this soup are special cells called imaginal discs, which use the food in the caterpillar soup to grow into all the parts of a butterfly.

2 FEBRUARY

B   When a butterfly lands on a plant, the chemoreceptors on its feet can detect whether the plant is sweet, bitter, sour or salty. And, when a butterfly lands on you, it's probably because they're tasting the sweat on your skin! Butterflies taste leaves to work out which one is best to lay eggs on.

3 FEBRUARY

C   Butterflies drink nectar from flowers, but they also eat blood, sweat and poop! They drink the tears of reptiles for the salt, blood and sweat, and they'll also eat soil, rotting plants, urine and rotten animals.

4 FEBRUARY

A Butterflies have lots of vibrant colours on their wings for a couple of reasons. First of all, the colours tell predators that the butterfly might be poisonous and yucky to eat. Second, the colours also help butterflies to find a mate by allowing them to show them off when they are courting!

5 FEBRUARY

C There are two different types of tickling: knismesis is from a light touch and doesn't usually make us laugh, while gargalesis is the harder sort of tickling that does make us laugh. Knismesis helps us to notice when something unexpected touches our skin, like a mosquito, and gargalesis is thought to be an automatic defence mechanism that helps us to protect sensitive parts of our bodies, like our stomachs.

6 FEBRUARY

A We usually get the hiccups when we have eaten or drunk too much, or too quickly. The stomach becomes distended and irritates the diaphragm, which is just above it. (The diaphragm is the part of the body that goes in and out when breathing.) This causes the diaphragm to contract uncontrollably, making us breathe in – but quickly, so we go "HICCUP!" as it contracts.

7 FEBRUARY

A
+
B
+
C

The answer is a combination of all three! Practising tongue-rolling can make you better at making shapes with your tongue, but some people are naturally better at making shapes with their tongues. This comes down to lots of different factors, including the genes you've inherited from your parents, and the size and shape of your tongue.

8 FEBRUARY

B   The insides of our noses are made of very delicate tissues, and we produce mucus to moisturize and protect them. Cold, dry air can irritate these delicate tissues, so we produce more mucus than usual. Think of the mucus as an extra layer your body makes to keep your nose cosy!

9 FEBRUARY

A   It's a tradition in some Asian cultures to give red envelopes full of money at Lunar New Year, because red symbolizes energy and good luck. It's good to give new paper money, not old wrinkled-up money. People often go around with red envelopes full of cash in case they meet someone they ought to give a gift to. If someone

gives you one, accept it with both hands,
then open it at home in private, not in front
of the person who gave it to you.

10 FEBRUARY

C There are twelve animals in the Chinese zodiac:
the rat, the ox, the tiger, the rabbit, the dragon,
the snake, the horse, the goat, the monkey,
the rooster, the dog and the pig. This quiz book
was published in 2024, the Year of the Dragon,
also known as Year of the Loong. The dragon is
the fifth animal in the twelve-year cycle.

11 FEBRUARY

A On the fifteenth day of Lunar New Year
celebrations, it's time for the Lantern Festival,
during which people in China and other Asian
societies sometimes send lanterns up into
the sky. Some people think of the lanterns as
offerings to the Buddha, and sometimes you
write wishes on paper and tie them to the
lanterns, hoping the lanterns will take your
wishes up to the sky. Releasing the lanterns is a
way of celebrating hope, saying goodbye to bad
things, letting light into your life, remembering
people you love and wishing for a happy future.

12 FEBRUARY

C   The Egyptians thought that, when a person died, their spirit left their body. So, they wrapped the body up to protect it, so the owner could use it again in the afterlife.

13 FEBRUARY

B   When the driver of the car presses down on the gas pedal or accelerator, energy is sent through the different parts of the car in a "power train". Energy moves through the drive shaft – the part of the car that moves the energy from the engine to the wheels – to the axle – the pole connecting the wheels. Then, the wheels start turning and the car moves!

14 FEBRUARY

C   Some pipes feed the car the different liquids and gases that it needs to keep working, while other pipes pump out the fumes that the car needs to get rid of. There are lots of pipes inside a car, and they each have a different job! They pump in fuel to give the car energy to move, cooling fluids to keep it cool and washer fluid to clean the windshield! The pipes that pump out bad fumes produced by fuel are called exhaust pipes.

15 FEBRUARY

A To begin with, roads didn't have lines. People just knew which side to drive on – but on curves they sometimes veered over to the wrong side. So, it was decided that lines in the middle of roads were needed. The first line was put on a road in Wayne County, Michigan, in the United States of America, in 1911. The designer, Edward Hines, had the idea after watching a leaky milk truck go down the road spilling white milk.

16 FEBRUARY

A Sloths are the only mammals that cannot fart. Instead, they let go of gas out of their mouths!

17 FEBRUARY

C Skunks spray stinky chemicals out of glands on each side of their bottoms. They lift their tails to spray so that they don't spray themselves! Skunks only carry enough stinky chemical for five to six uses, and if they use it all up they need around ten days to refill their tanks. The main thing that creates the stinky smell is sulphur.

18 FEBRUARY

A   Often farts don't smell! This is because most of the gases our intestines make as they digest food – like carbon dioxide, nitrogen, hydrogen and methane – don't smell. But there is *one* gas we make that smells awful: hydrogen sulphide. It smells like rotten eggs! And it's what makes some farts smell bad. We produce hydrogen sulphide when we eat foods with sulphur in them, such as meat, broccoli, sprouts, cabbage, kale and cauliflower.

19 FEBRUARY

C   Hurricanes spin counterclockwise in the northern hemisphere, and clockwise in the southern hemisphere. This is because of how air currents flow in the different hemispheres.

20 FEBRUARY

A   Weather forecasters, or meteorologists, observe what's happening right now using kit such as radar, satellites and weather balloons. Supercomputers then use the information that forecasters have gathered to predict future weather, and meteorologists constantly update it and change the forecasts. We can make good guesses by looking at the wind and the sky, too, though!

21 FEBRUARY

A   The Pan-American Highway is the longest road in the world, and it stretches nearly 30,000 miles (48,300 kilometres) from the north of Alaska all the way to Argentina.

22 FEBRUARY

A   The world's longest bridge is China's Danyang–Kunshan Grand Bridge, which is 103 miles (165 kilometres) long. It's part of the Beijing–Shanghai high-speed railway, and it took four years to build.

23 FEBRUARY

C   The optic nerve at the back of the eyeball connects the eye to the brain, and it's this nerve that keeps the eyeball in place. There is also a bone in the eye socket to hold it steady.

24 FEBRUARY

C   When you cut an onion, it releases chemicals that mix together to create another chemical called syn-Propanethial-S-oxide, which is lighter than air and floats up to your eyes. Your brain then picks up the danger of having this chemical near your eyes, and tells the glands in your eyes to make tears to wash it out!

25 FEBRUARY

A   All the fluids in our body contain a little salt, which is made into electricity to help our muscles and our brains to work. Tears are just one of the fluids in our body. There's also sweat, saliva and blood, and they all also contain salt. Did you know that tears you cry when you are happy or sad contain less salt than the ones your eyes cry to clean themselves or keep moist?

26 FEBRUARY

A   Yes, you can cry underwater – although the water will wash your tears away quickly.

27 FEBRUARY

C   Scallops have up to 200 eyes! Their eyes are like telescopes, and each one has two retinas so the scallop can see narrow and peripheral (side-on) views at the same time.

28 FEBRUARY

C   "Happy Birthday to You" was written in 1893 by two sisters, Mildred and Patty Hill, in Kentucky, in the United States of America. It was first called *"Good Morning to You"* and went like this: *"Good morning to you. Good morning to you.*

Good morning, dear children. Good morning to all!" Then the words changed to say "happy birthday". It might be the most commonly sung song in the English-speaking world!

29 FEBRUARY

A   Leap years occur every four years, and add a twenty-ninth day to the month of February so that the year has 366 days instead of 365. We have leap years because of the time it takes the Earth to orbit the Sun – 365 and a quarter days. This means that, every four years, we have to add all the extra quarter days together to make a full day, to make sure we don't slowly go out of sync with the seasons!

1 MARCH

B Phones get text messages using wireless communication, known as Wi-Fi. When you send a message, it is called data. A cellular tower or Wi-Fi router picks up this data, and sends it to another phone, where it is turned back into a text message.

2 MARCH

A When you press a button on a remote control, it completes an electrical circuit. The remote then makes a signal which is picked up by a receiver in the TV. Infrared remotes use light to communicate, whereas radio frequency remotes use radio frequency signals.

3 MARCH

C Released in 1972, the Magnavox Odyssey was the first games console. It came in a box with a board game, cards, paper money and dice to help you play the game.

4 MARCH

C Although sheep are the best producers of wool, other animals can also produce it – including dogs! Wool made from dog fur is called chiengora. Newfoundland dogs have lots of fur, and just brushing these dogs gives you lots of fur that can be spun into wool, then knitted into whatever you like. Maybe a hat?

5 MARCH

C Dogs have fur to keep their bodies just the right temperature – not too hot, and not too cold. Their fur also protects them from cuts and scratches.

6 MARCH

A Dogs have lots of things called sensory receptor sites in their nose that help them to smell. While humans have about 6 million sensory receptor sites, dogs have up to 300 million! The part of a dog's brain that picks up smell is also 40 times bigger than the same part of a human's brain. Dogs also sniff all the time, and can wiggle their nostrils in different directions at the same time.

7 MARCH

C *Digitalis* means "finger-like" and refers to the foxglove's long flowers.

8 MARCH

C   *Archaefructus* was white, and looked a bit like a water lily and a magnolia mixed together. It could be one of the first flowering plants, and grew around 130 million years ago in China, probably near the water.

9 MARCH

B   A single sunflower head may contain up to 2,000 seeds.

10 MARCH

B   Dumbledore is an old English word that used to mean "bumblebee".

11 MARCH

C   Bananas probably came from the jungles of Malaysia, Indonesia and the Philippines in Southeast Asia. They were spread across Asia by travellers, then to Africa, where they got their name from the Arabic word for finger!

12 MARCH

C   The first person to grow bananas in Europe was Carl Linnaeus, a Swedish scientist who also came up with a way to name species. Copying the monsoon climates of Asia, he let the soil dry out, then bombarded the banana plant with water. He then presented his banana crop to the King of Sweden.

13 MARCH

B   The appendix is the thin tube attached to the gut, and some scientists believe that it could help us to fight infections.

14 MARCH

A   Most pen companies say the average pen could draw a line of up to 2 miles (3 kilometres), which is the length of 125 tennis courts.

15 MARCH

C   Helium is found in pockets under the Earth's surface, and it is lighter than air. So, a balloon filled with helium will float in the air.

16 MARCH

B We grow hair in our armpits for a couple of
+ reasons. First, it stops the skin rubbing when
C we run and walk. Second, when we sweat, our
bodies make chemicals called pheromones that
can attract other humans – and sweat attaches to
armpit hair!

17 MARCH

A Vomiting is the body's way of getting rid of
things that could do us harm. It could be a virus
or bacteria from a bug that is going around, or it
could be food poisoning from eating food that
has gone bad.

18 MARCH

C Human blood is red because it contains a protein
called haemoglobin, which has a red-coloured
compound in it called heme that carries oxygen
around the body.

19 MARCH

C A healthy adult has about 35 trillion red blood
cells. Our bodies make an incredible 2.4 million
new blood cells every second! These red blood

cells carry oxygen all over our bodies. White blood cells, which help fight infection, make up only 1 per cent of our blood.

20 MARCH

B If you took all of the blood vessels out of an adult and laid them in a line, they would be close to 60,000 miles (96,560 kilometres) long. That's enough to circle the Earth more than twice! Or, to put it another way, it's like travelling from London all the way round the Earth 2.4 times.

21 MARCH

B Greyhounds are the fastest breed of dog, and can run up to 45 miles (72 kilometres) per hour. That's almost twice as fast as the current fastest person in the world, Usain Bolt, has run!

22 MARCH

B Tails help dogs to balance, move and communicate. Puppies don't wag their tails until they're around 30 days old, which is when they start learning to "speak" to one another! Some dogs even use their tails to steer when they swim, like a boat's rudder.

23 MARCH

C The biggest ant colonies in the world are supercolonies made by the Argentine ant, an invasive species from South America, and they contain billions of ants! In Europe, there is a 3,700-mile-long supercolony (6,000 kilometres) that stretches along the coasts of Portugal, Spain, France and Italy, and it is filled with millions of interconnected nests and billions of ants.

24 MARCH

B Turtles are relatively voiceless, so we don't hear much from them. The one thing we do hear, though, is heavy breathing. When they are nesting, you'll hear turtles making big sighing sounds, breathing in and out.

25 MARCH

C Adult male turtles have longer tails than adult females do.

26 MARCH

B All creatures need to sleep.

27 MARCH

A   The King's Imperial State Crown weighs a little more than 1 kilogram. It is made of gold, and has 2,868 diamonds, four rubies, eleven emeralds, seventeen sapphires and 269 pearls.

28 MARCH

B   Queen Elizabeth II took the throne at the age of just 25, and ended up reigning for over 70 years – the longest of any king or queen of England ever!

29 MARCH

A   The highest recorded jump over a bar by a guinea pig was 24 centimetres. The jump was made by Willow the guinea pig in Madrid, in Spain, on 14 January 2023. When guinea pigs are really happy, they do little leaps of joy. This is called popcorning, because they look like popcorn popping and flying into the air! Another fun thing they do are zoomies – running around with a big burst of energy. *Zooooom!*

30 MARCH

B The climate of Hawai'i is the same as the hamster's native climate, plus hamsters make babies really quickly. This means that hamsters could easily spread all over Hawai'i and threaten lots of native animals, so that's why they're illegal there.

31 MARCH

A When we get hot we sweat, which helps to cool our skin. However, pigs don't have many sweat glands, so they roll in mud to keep cool! This also helps to protect their skin from sunburn and parasites.

1 APRIL

C The heaviest chocolate bar in the world was made in Derbyshire, in England, in 2011. It was 4 metres by 4 metres in size, 35 centimetres thick and weighed 5,792 kilograms. It would have been hard to bite!

2 APRIL

A Here is one way to make chocolate spread! Get a grown-up to help you roast some hazelnuts in the oven, then remove their skins and blend them in a food processor or blender until they turn into nut butter. Add some cocoa powder, icing sugar, sunflower oil and melted chocolate, and mix it all together, then pop it in the fridge to cool.

3 APRIL

B Germany makes more chocolate than any other country in the world. Four countries – Germany, Belgium, Italy and Poland – produce over 40 per cent of the world's chocolate! However, most of the world's supply of cacao, which is the main ingredient in chocolate, is actually grown throughout Africa. Most is grown in Côte d'Ivoire, which produces around 30 per cent of the world's cacao beans.

4 APRIL

B   In 1847, Joseph Fry, from Bristol in England, made the first mass-produced chocolate bar. He worked out how to mix cocoa powder, sugar and cocoa to make a paste to mould into a bar.

5 APRIL

B   Many reptiles cry, including crocodiles, but not because they're sad. They cry because the tears clean out and protect their eyes. We think the only animals that cry because they're emotional are humans! When we say someone is crying "crocodile tears", we mean that they are pretending to cry in order to get what they want.

6 APRIL

B   Crocodiles live in the water in parts of Africa, Asia, Australia, Central America, the West Indies and northern South America.

7 APRIL

A   The Tárcoles River in Costa Rica has around 2,000 crocodiles living in it! So don't swim in it if you ever happen to visit. There is a big bridge over it where you can look down at the crocodiles from the safety of the road.

8 APRIL

A   The giant armadillo's claws are 20 centimetres long, making them the longest-clawed living animal. If you included dinosaurs, though, the *Therizinosaurus* would win! Its claws measured 91 centimetres long.

9 APRIL

A   Humans take around 20,000 breaths each day. That's about 7.3 million breaths a year!

10 APRIL

C   Lots of families teach their babies simple sign language when they're around six months old, so that they can tell the grown-ups what they want rather than crying. Babies and caregivers can learn the signs for "milk", "hugs" and "too hot" or "too cold". How clever is that!

11 APRIL

B   Gravity and speed keep the Moon in place. In fact, the Moon is always falling towards the Earth, but it is moving so fast and is so far away that it will never hit our planet. Instead, it falls *round* the Earth, in a continuous path called an orbit – it orbits the Earth just as the Earth orbits the Sun. If the Moon were moving faster, it would escape Earth's gravity and fly off into space. If it were moving more slowly, gravity would pull it down to Earth. The Moon has the perfect balance of speed and gravity to create an orbit.

12 APRIL

C When a bat gives birth, it catches its baby in its wings. Then, the baby bat clings on and drinks milk, all upside down. At around three weeks old, bat babies learn to fly. By six weeks, they can catch their own insects to eat, so join the adult bats when they go hunting at night, then hang upside down all day.

13 APRIL

A Bats aren't blind! They actually have good eyesight. And they're very confused about why people keep saying they're "blind as a bat". Bats have small eyes and sensitive vision, so they can see even in the dark! They can't see colour like we can, but they don't need to.

14 APRIL

B Anglerfish are best known for the lure above their heads that lights up in the deep sea to attract other fish so that the anglerfish can then gobble them up! Female anglerfish can live up to 25 years, but males tend to live to around 20 years. It's quite hard to study anglerfish, as they live so deep in the ocean, but that's what scientists think so far.

15 APRIL

B   The Pacific is the world's oldest ocean basin, and the oldest rocks on the bottom are around 200 million years old. But it is shrinking in size by a few centimetres each year, as the Atlantic Ocean expands, because the great plates of the Earth's crust move around a little all the time.

16 APRIL

C   The common dolphin is the fastest marine mammal, and can swim at 37 miles (60 kilometres) per hour. An orca's top speed isn't far off that, at 34 miles (55.5 kilometres) per hour – but that's during a short burst. Usually, orcas travel at around 4–5 miles (6–8 kilometres) per hour. Meanwhile, the fastest a blue whale can swim is 31 miles (50 kilometres) per hour.

17 APRIL

A   The tallest coast redwood tree in the world is named Hyperion, and stands 115.92 metres tall – nearly the same height as the Centre Point building in London, in England. Coast redwood trees usually reach around 107 metres in height.

18 APRIL

B   Trees pull carbon dioxide out of the air. In a way, they "breathe" it in through little holes in their leaves called stomata. They then use sunlight to turn that carbon dioxide into sugars that they use to build wood, branches and roots. This whole process is called photosynthesis. Oxygen is made during photosynthesis, and the tree releases this oxygen out into the air.

19 APRIL

A   More than 70 per cent of the Earth's oxygen is produced by plants that live in the ocean. It is made by tiny marine plants, plankton and some bacteria. One bacteria called *prochlorococcus* is so tiny we can't see it – and it makes 20 per cent of the oxygen on Earth!

20 APRIL

C   There are about 1,260 million trillion litres of water in all Earth's oceans.

21 APRIL

C   A fish's scales protect its body in much the same way as a suit of armour would. If the fish crashes into coral or is attacked by a predator, the scales help to defend it.

22 APRIL

C   Baby swans are called cygnets, and weigh around 250 grams and are 20 centimetres long when they hatch. Six months later, they will be around 6 kilograms, but it takes three or four years for them to reach their full adult weight and size.

23 APRIL

B   Genes determine the traits passed on to offspring from their parents. The gene that makes the orange colour in a ginger cat is on the X chromosome. Females have two X chromosomes, so need two copies of this gene to be ginger, whereas males need only one.

24 APRIL

A Experts believe that each cat can create more than 60 meows. Kittens use their meows to communicate with their mothers, while older cats meow at humans to communicate with them – to say, for example, that they're hungry or unhappy.

25 APRIL

C Cats hiss when they feel threatened or worried. It's their way of saying, "Leave me alone or I might attack you!" They're hoping the hissing will make you or another cat back off.

26 APRIL

C The golden poison arrow frog is the deadliest in the world, and its skin makes a poison that can paralyse and kill! It lives in the forests and rainforests along the Pacific coast of Colombia, and is very important to the Indigenous people of the area. They use the frog's poison on the darts they use to hunt their food, and the darts' tips remain deadly for years!

27 APRIL

A The mosquito is the deadliest animal in the world. It carries diseases that kill around one million people a year. By contrast, sharks only kill around ten people a year and crocodiles around 1,500.

28 APRIL

C   Spiders make two types of silk: sticky and non-sticky. They try not to walk on the sticky bits of their web. They also have claws on their feet to grip the web as they go.

29 APRIL

C   Spiders hatch out of eggs! Female spiders lay eggs on a bed of silk, cover them in a silk blanket, then wrap them safely in a silk egg sac. When the baby spiders are ready to be born, they hatch out of the eggs.

30 APRIL

C   Spiders do not sleep in the same way we do. They don't have eyelids, so they can't close their eyes. Instead, they rest and slow down their body functions to save energy. You know when you shut a laptop and it turns off, but then if you open it again and press a key it will spring back to life? Spiders are a bit like that!

1 MAY

C Sloths eat food that hasn't got much energy in it, so they move slowly to save energy. Moving slowly also means predators don't notice them very easily.

2 MAY

C Sloths, anteaters and armadillos are all part of an ancient group of mammals called xenarthrans. These animals share distinctive features including large curved claws and strong limbs for digging.

3 MAY

B Inside a piano is a row of strings, and below that is a row of little felt-covered hammers. When you press a key, the hammer linked to that key hits the string below – or the strings, if it's above two or three. The string or strings then vibrate, making a note! Each string is stretched to vibrate at a different speed, which is why they make different notes.

4 MAY

B The main type of protein in milk is called casein, and it clumps together into little globules called micelles. When light hits these micelles, all of the light is reflected, rather than some being absorbed. That means we see *all* the colours in the light, which looks white to us!

5 MAY

C Egg yolks are made of protein, fat, lecithin and carotenoid. Lecithin is what's called an emulsifier, meaning it helps things mix together. Carotenoid comes from the hens' food, and it gives the yolks their yellowy colour!

6 MAY

A Bees sting to defend themselves. They only sting if they feel threatened, for instance if they are going to get trodden on or someone is trying to attack their hive.

7 MAY

A Sort of. Bees have six parts to their legs: the coxa, the trochanter, the femur, the tibia, the metatarsus and the tarsus. Each part is connected to the next by a joint – so, in a way, bees have several knees!

8 MAY

B   The queen is usually the only bee in the hive that lays eggs, so she is very important.

9 MAY

B   The very first apples came from Kazakhstan, in Central Asia. Its former capital is called Almaty, which means "full of apples".

10 MAY

A   Orange the fruit came first! Orange was used to describe fruit in the fourteenth century, and as a colour later in the 1510s.

11 MAY

C   Unripe fruit is green because of a substance called chlorophyll in its cells. As the fruit ripens, the chlorophyll breaks down and is replaced by orange carotenoids and red anthocyanins. These substances help the fruit to stay ripe, rather than go off quickly – and the colours also show animals and humans that the fruit is ripe!

12 MAY

C   You call more than one banana a hand,
while individual bananas are called fingers!

13 MAY

A   Delicious bananas aren't the only part
of the banana plant that you can eat.
Banana flowers are really popular as a food in
Southeast Asia, and you can also eat the green
trunk of the plant. It tastes good when it is
cooked in coconut milk.

14 MAY

C   Snails can sleep for up to three years – that's
94,608,000 seconds! They need moisture to
survive, so if it's too hot and there isn't enough
water they go into hibernation, and sleep until
the weather's more snail-friendly.

15 MAY

B   Slugs don't have ears, so they can't hear sound.
Instead, they sense their environment through
smell, taste, sight and touch.

16 MAY

B   Beetle blood is clear, or tinged yellow or green. Insect blood doesn't have red cells in it, so it isn't red like our blood. When a fly is squashed and red liquid appears, that's pigment from its eyes!

17 MAY

B   The bootlace worm (*Lineus longissimus*) is the longest species of worm, and the longest measured was found in Scotland after a storm. It was over 55 metres long – nearly as tall as the Leaning Tower of Pisa!

18 MAY

C   When bees make honey, they gather nectar from flowers. Nectar contains sugar and water, and plants make it very sweet so that creatures will drink it and spread the plants' pollen to make new plants!

19 MAY

C   Plants need water for all of these reasons! First, they need it for photosynthesis, which is how they make their own food – for this process, they need water along with sunlight and carbon dioxide from the air. Water also helps plants to keep cool in the heat, and it supports their cells to keep them strong and flexible.

20 MAY

C   The largest individual flower in the world is the corpse flower (*Rafflesia arnoldii*). It is native to Indonesia and grows to nearly 1 metre wide! It gets its name from its strong smell, which attracts the insects that pollinate it and is similar to rotting flesh. Yuck!

21 MAY

B   Space begins at least 50 miles (80 kilometres) above the ground, so a tree would have to grow at least that high to reach space! Redwoods are some of the tallest trees in the world, and the tallest living one reaches only 115.92 metres high.

22 MAY

C   The oldest living thing that is still alive is a form of bacteria. Scientists found it inside salt crystals and it is 250 million years old! Other very old living organisms include the clonal tree Pando in Utah, in the United States of America, whose root system could be 80,000 years old, and a bristlecone pine tree that is 5,000 years old in California, in the United States of America.

23 MAY

C   The fifteenth day of the first Tibetan month of the year is the last day of Tibetan New Year, and it's known as the Monlam Festival or Butter Lantern Festival. On that day, Tibetans eat delicious pastries and sweet rice, and send lanterns fuelled by yak butter into the sky. They make statues out of coloured butter as prayers, and there is lots of singing, dancing and puppet shows. Sounds fun!

24 MAY

A   There are way more chickens in the world than humans! Billions and billions more, in fact. As of the year 2023, we think there were about 34.4 billion chickens, but it's quite hard to count them, even when they've hatched.

25 MAY

C   Ladybirds have spots for protection, as the spots make them look yucky to predators. Spots indicate that they will taste unpleasant, and could be poisonous.

26 MAY

B   When leaves are green, they absorb sunlight and turn it into sugars for the tree. Chlorophyll is the substance that helps them to do this, and also makes the leaves green. When there is less sunlight – during winter, for instance – some trees store the chlorophyll, then shed their leaves. By doing this, they save energy and can survive the winter.

27 MAY

C Snails produce a sticky slime called mucus, which creates suction and makes them stick to a leaf – even when they are upside down!

28 MAY

A Chameleons change colour depending
+ on their mood, their environment, the
B light around them and their temperature.
+ They also do it to attract mates to
C breed with!

29 MAY

C Geckos don't have eyelids, so they can't blink. Instead, they use their tongue to clean their eyeballs!

30 MAY

B The Megalania was 6 metres long, and was likely the largest venomous animal to have ever lived! We think that it ate mammals, reptiles and birds, and that early humans lived alongside it in Australia. These days, the biggest lizard is the Komodo dragon, which can grow to as long as 3.13 metres. These dragons live in Komodo, an island in Indonesia, and on other little islands nearby.

31 MAY

C Komodo dragons eat meat, from rodents to water buffalo. They can smell potential prey from 2.5 miles (4 kilometres) away, using their forked tongue and a special walk where they swing their head from side to side. If they pick up more scent on the left tongue fork than on the right, they know an animal must be nearby on the left.

1 JUNE

C The National Oceanic and Atmospheric Administration (NOAA) thinks there are at least a million sunken ships on the bottom of the ocean, so there could be billions of pounds' worth of treasure down there! It won't be gold coins, like in books and films about pirates, but treasure in terms of all kinds of objects.

2 JUNE

B At 10,930 metres, Challenger Deep is the deepest part of the Mariana Trench, which is located in the Pacific Ocean between Hawai'i and the Philippines.

3 JUNE

A The biggest ocean island in the world is Greenland, in the Arctic.

4 JUNE

B Sponges are made of loose fibres with spaces, or holes, in between. If you put a sponge in water, the holes will absorb the water, and the sponge swells up until it's full.

5 JUNE

A Bark protects a tree's trunk and branches, a bit like a hard skin.

6 JUNE

A In spring and summer, leaves contain chlorophyll, which makes them green. Plants use chlorophyll to turn sunlight into food. In autumn, there is less sun, so some plants break down the chlorophyll to get out the nutrients and store them for winter. The chemicals left behind are what give the leaves an orange or yellow colour.

7 JUNE

B Humans drink water because we have to. Our bodies won't work without it! We need water to survive.

8 JUNE

A Scientists believe that wrinkly skin in the bath is caused by the top layers of the skin swelling and/or the lower layers shrinking when we're in water for a long time. They think this happens so that our fingers can get a better grip and things won't slip out of our hands. It's a bit like the lumpy tread on a car tyre!

9 JUNE

A   Our eyes are covered with a liquid layer that keeps them happy during the day. At night, when we sleep with our eyes closed, this layer is protected and our eyes are given lots of moisture. If we stay awake too long, then the layer begins to evaporate a bit, which makes our eyes dry out and get bloodshot.

10 JUNE

A   Even newborn giraffes are taller than most adult humans! A baby giraffe is around 1.8 metres tall, while the average male human is only 1.7 metres and average female 1.6 metres.

11 JUNE

C   The biggest animal baby belongs to the blue whale! Newborn blue whales weigh 2,722 kilograms – as heavy as pick-up truck.

12 JUNE

B   It takes around a year for elephants to work out how to drink using their trunk. Baby elephants spend ages splashing water around while they're getting the hang of it! Until they do work it out, they drink through their mouths, usually by bending their front legs right down and sticking their head in a pool of water. Did you know that elephants can also use their trunks to snorkel? They stick their trunks out of the water to breathe when they're swimming across big rivers!

13 JUNE

B
+
C
Humans are not the only thumb-suckers! Chimpanzees, lemurs in zoos and other primates do it, too, and newborn elephants suck their trunks if they want to comfort themselves. Adult elephants also calm themselves down with their trunks by touching their faces, which helps them to relax.

14 JUNE

A An elephant's legs are very long, and its head is large and heavy, so bending down to eat and drink can be tiring! Its long trunk helps it to get food without moving its head, and to keep eating while grabbing more food.

15 JUNE

C The Middlemist's red camellia was imported from China to England by a man named John Middlemist. Only two of these flowers remain in

the world – one in New Zealand, and
the other in Chiswick House and Gardens
in the United Kingdom.

16 JUNE

B   Pluto is a lot further from the Sun than we
are here on Earth, so it's a lot colder there!
The average temperature on Pluto is a very
chilly –232°C, which is much too cold for any
living thing to survive.

17 JUNE

A   If you were to jump into a black hole,
the gravity force would compress you while
also stretching you, leaving you looking a little
like strings of spaghetti!

18 JUNE

B   The diameter of the Sun is about 870,000 miles
(1.4 million kilometres). It is the largest object in
the solar system, and it's so big you could line up
109 Earths across its face!

19 JUNE

C   Point Nemo, in the southern Pacific Ocean, is 1,000 miles (1,600 kilometres) from the coasts of its three closest islands: Ducie Island, Moto Nui and Maher Island. It's so far away that, if you were there, you might be closer to an astronaut in space than to another human on Earth!

20 JUNE

C   Tiny little crustaceans called Antarctic krill are the most abundant animal species on Earth. There are more of them than any other animal we know of!

21 JUNE

B   Nauru is an island country in the Pacific, and it has no official capital.

22 JUNE

C   Although it's impossible to say exactly which food humans made first, we can tell from bone remains at some of the oldest archaeological sites that it might have been cooked meat.

23 JUNE

C   Sunlight looks white, but is actually made up of all the colours of the rainbow. When it reaches the Earth's atmosphere, it scatters. Blue light scatters the most, and that is why the sky looks blue!

24 JUNE

A   Clouds are made of hundreds of thousands of tiny water droplets. There's lots of water in the air that you can't see because it's a gas, but when the air cools this water comes together and forms clouds. Rain is made in clouds when they grow tall and begin to look dark and grey – the water droplets at the top freeze and grow bigger, then fall and pass through the warmer air below and start to melt. And it rains!

25 JUNE

C   The wind carries clouds through the air. Even when it seems there is no wind down on the ground, it can be windy higher in the atmosphere.

26 JUNE

B The longest reign by a monarch of a sovereign state was Louis XIV of France. He ruled for 72 years and 110 days, from 1643 until 1715. Queen Elizabeth II of England, who died in 2022, was the United Kingdom's monarch for more than 70 years. Tutankhamun was an ancient Egyptian pharaoh who ruled for just nine years, and died at the age of about eighteen in the year 1323 BCE.

27 JUNE

B The so-called Reconquista was a 781-year period of conflict from the year 711 to 1492, when Christian kingdoms in Spain and Portugal fought with the Muslim Moors for control of the Iberian Peninsula.

28 JUNE

B Sand can be made from different things that are broken down over time into tiny pieces, including rocks, bits of skeleton and shells. It can also be made when parrotfish poo! Parrotfish eat coral and poo out the rocky calcium carbonate they don't digest. This can form entire beaches!

ANSWERS

29 JUNE

A The first wave riders we know of lived in ancient Polynesia. The first surfboards were made of wood, and surfing was part of local culture and mythology.

30 JUNE

B A tortoise can feel every scratch or rub or tap on its shell, because its shell has lots of nerve endings.

1 JULY

A   A blue whale's heartbeat can drop to just two beats per minute, while the Etruscan shrew's heart beats up to 1,500 times per minute. A human's heart beats, on average, 70 times per minute.

2 JULY

C   Dolphins sleep while they swim! Since they are mammals, they can't breathe underwater, so they still need to come to the surface to breathe while they're asleep. To do this, they sleep with one half of their brain at a time – the half that stays awake tells the dolphin when it needs to swim to the surface to take a new breath.

3 JULY

C   A sailfish is the fastest fish in the world, and can swim 68 miles (110 kilometres) per hour. That's as fast as a cheetah, the fastest creature on land!

4 JULY

A   A giraffe's tail is the longest on land, and is around 2.4 metres long. In the sea, the largest tail belongs to the blue whale. Its tail is known as a fluke, and is 7.5 metres wide.

5 JULY

B Bonobos may have been called that by mistake! They live near a town called Bolobo in the Democratic Republic of the Congo, in Africa, and it's believed that, back in the twentieth century, the town's name was written on a crate carrying a bonobo to Germany. When the crate got to Germany, the scientists who opened it thought the name referred to the animal inside – but they misspelled it as "bonobo". So they got the meaning *and* the spelling wrong!

6 JULY

A Nest is best! Orangutans, like gorillas, make nests to sleep in out of branches and leaves. It takes them around ten minutes to make a new nest every night.

7 JULY

B Orangutans in the wild have an average lifespan of 30–40 years. In captivity, they can live longer, into their fifties. Did you know that the scientific name for an orangutan is *Pongo*?

8 JULY

B The idea of dragons or dragon-like creatures have been around for as long as we know. Perhaps ancient people discovered dinosaur bones, whale bones, fossilized crocodiles or monitor lizards and thought they were dragons? One thing we do know is that dragons have been in folk tales and myths from all around the world for so long that it's not possible to find the first one.

9 JULY

A Megalodon was an enormous shark measuring 15–18 metres long – that's three times longer than the largest great white! Archaeologists have found megalodon as old as 20 million years. The megalodon had 276 teeth, and these could be 18 centimetres long, which explains the shark's name – megalodon means "large tooth". Its bite was 100 times more powerful than a human's!

10 JULY

C Teeth are made of pulp, dentin, enamel and cementum. Pulp contains nerves, blood vessels and tissues that connect and support other tissues. Dentin is the hard substance that surrounds the pulp, while enamel is the hard tissue on the tooth. Cementum is what holds the tooth in place!

11 JULY

C   The femur, or thigh bone, is the longest bone in the human body. The longest femur ever recorded belonged to a German man known as Constantine the Giant, and it was 76 centimetres in length.

12 JULY

C   The skin is the heaviest organ in the human body, and it is also the largest! Our skin is a barrier between us and the world.

13 JULY

C   Our lips hold food in our mouths while we're eating, and we can suck with them – this is especially important when we are babies, so that we can breastfeed or drink from a bottle. They also help us to communicate with kisses, smiles and by making sounds such as "p".

14 JULY

B   The Sun isn't yellow. It's white! If you looked at the Sun from the Moon, it would be white. The reason it looks yellow during the day, or red or orange at sunrise and sunset, here on Earth is because we see the Sun through the filter of our planet's atmosphere.

15 JULY

C There are plenty of stars behind the Sun, but we can't usually see them during the day because of the bright blue sky or the clouds. We can, however, see them in daytime during a total solar eclipse, because the sky turns dark. In 1919, Arthur Eddington went to Príncipe, an island in the Democratic Republic of São Tomé and Príncipe, off the western coast of Central Africa. There, he used a huge telescope to take photographs of starlight shining from behind the Sun during a solar eclipse, and these photos showed starlight bending around the Sun!

16 JULY

C If an aeroplane were able to fly to the Moon, it would take seventeen days of non-stop flying to get there.

17 JULY

B The stars don't move. We do! The Earth is moving and spinning in space, and we move with it. So, it looks like the stars, the Sun and the Moon are moving across the sky, but actually it's us here on the Earth moving.

18 JULY

B   When baby wombats are born, they are the size of a jellybean. They crawl straight into their mother's pouch, and stay there to grow for six to ten months.

19 JULY

C   Koalas sleep for 20 hours a day, making them the sleepiest animals in the world. Sloths and tigers need sixteen hours of sleep, goats need five hours, and giraffes need only two and a half hours! Giraffes sometimes lie down to sleep, but mostly they sleep standing up and resting their heads on their bottoms.

20 JULY

C   Wobbegongs, otherwise known as carpet sharks, inhabit the waters at the bottom of the Pacific and Indian Oceans. Their name is said to have come from a word meaning "shaggy beard", because of the fringe-like lobes round its head.

21 JULY

C   Marsupials usually carry their young in a pouch, and include kangaroos, koalas, Tasmanian devils, wombats, wallabies and bandicoots. Nowadays, they live in Australasia and the Americas, but the biggest marsupial ever isn't around any more. It was called the diprotodon, a name that comes from the ancient Greek for "two sticky-out front teeth", and was similar in size to a hippo. Diprotodons walked across Australia, eating plants with their big teeth and strong jaws, and moving with the seasons in big herds. It's possible the females carried their babies backwards in their pouches, like wombats do. They went extinct about 46,000 years ago, along with every other Australian animal over 100 kilograms – probably because there was no water, and humans started to hunt them as they had nothing else to eat.

22 JULY

B If you were invisible, light would go right through you. There'd be no light bouncing off you, so no one could see you – but the light would also go right through your eyes, so *you* wouldn't be able to see anything, either!

23 JULY

B Sound waves are reflected off hard surfaces, a bit like a ball being bounced against a wall. If you're in an enclosed space, such as a cave or a big hall, there are multiple hard surfaces for sound waves to be reflected off. So, if you speak or make a noise in an enclosed space, the sound bounces around – and this is what makes an echo!

ANSWERS

24 JULY

B Shadows form when light (such as from the Sun) hits an object it cannot travel through (such as a tree or your body). When you see your shadow on a sunny day, your body has blocked the light from the Sun!

25 JULY

A Female bald eagles are larger than males, and also have longer wingspans. A female's average wingspan is about 2.1 metres, while a male's is about 1.9 metres. That's around the same length as some surfboards!

26 JULY

C Vultures usually live for anywhere from ten to 47 years, depending on the species. There are 22 species of vulture, and they all live for different amounts of time.

27 JULY

C Gravity is a force of attraction between two objects. We experience the gravity of our planet, which pulls us towards its centre. Since the Earth's centre is below our feet, it feels like we're being pulled down!

28 JULY

B   The reticulated python is the longest snake in the world. It grows up to about seven metres long – that's the average height of a giraffe!

29 JULY

C   It depends on the species of snake. Most of a snake's body is rib cage – snakes have between 104 and 150 vertebrae in the main part of their body! Their tails are made of anywhere between 10 and 205, depending on the size and shape of the snake.

30 JULY

C   Snakes don't have eyelids, so they can't blink.

31 JULY

C   The oldest intact rocks on Earth are believed to be found in the Acasta gneisses, which lie southeast of Great Bear Lake in Canada's Northwest Territories. There, rocks have been found that are estimated to be 4.28 billion years old.

1 AUGUST

C If you buy a badminton shuttlecock in a toyshop, it might be made from plastic. If you play professionally, however, the shuttlecock is made from feathers taken from the wing of a goose! A shuttlecock has feathers from either the goose's left wing or its right wing – but never from both, as feathers from each wing are shaped differently.

2 AUGUST

B In 1896, the modern Olympic Games were held in Athens, marking the first Olympics for more than 1,500 years. The first modern champion was American James Connolly, who won the triple jump.

3 AUGUST

B The name cricket comes from *krick*, an old Middle Dutch word that meant "stick". The Middle Dutch phrase for hockey was *met de krik ket sen*, which means "with the stick chase" – and *krik ket* sounds a lot like cricket!

4 AUGUST

C   The Japanese spider crab is the largest crab in the world. Its body measures 30 centimetres across, but its legs can be 3.4 metres from claw to claw. That's as long as a male polar bear!

5 AUGUST

A   Coconut crabs use their claws to scrape away the outside of a coconut, and this can take them hours or even days! They then stab the coconut at a weak spot, and rip it open. Eating coconuts helps these crabs to grow big – those that eat coconuts can grow larger than those that don't! Coconut crabs also eat fruits, plants and dead animals. They'll even eat their own exoskeleton – the hard covering of their body, which they shed as they grow – and other coconut crabs!

6 AUGUST

C   Jaguars have 30 teeth, which they use for attacking and eating prey. They have very strong jaw muscles, and a bite that's more powerful than that of any other big cat. They can even bite through crocodile skin and turtle shells!

7 AUGUST

A Sharks don't need to clean their teeth, because their teeth contain fluoride, a substance that makes teeth strong (which is why it's in our toothpaste!). This means sharks don't get cavities in their teeth. They also lose their teeth all the time, but they grow back. Sometimes, sharks do get a bit of tooth-cleaning help from wrasses, which are little fish that pick out and eat the bits of food left on sharks' teeth. Yum!

8 AUGUST

B How many teeth a shark has depends on what kind of shark it is, but on average sharks have anywhere between 50 and 300 teeth at a time. Unlike humans, sharks don't grow teeth and keep them. Instead, they have lots of rows of teeth, and when an old tooth drops out a new one replaces it – a bit like a conveyor belt of teeth!

9 AUGUST

B Our eyebrows protect our eyes, and they also help us to express ourselves! They stop things like rainwater and sweat from getting into our eyes and making it hard to see, but we can also move them around to express feelings, such as anger or surprise, without speaking.

10 AUGUST

A   Freckles form when the body makes too much melanin, and they are caused by the Sun. Melanin is a pigment that gives our hair, skin and eyes their colour, and our bodies make it to protect our skin from sun damage.

11 AUGUST

A   When we fall over, small veins and even tinier capillaries under the skin can burst. When this happens, blood leaks out but remains under the skin, forming a bruise that looks bluish, purplish, reddish or blackish from the outside.

12 AUGUST

A   Watermelons are 92 per cent water. A watermelon takes around 90 days to grow, from planting a seed to picking the fruit when it's ripe.

13 AUGUST

C   Ice cream is a solid, a liquid and a gas all at the same time! The ice crystals are solid, the milk and sugar are liquid, and the air bubbles are gas. Maybe that's why it is so delicious!

14 AUGUST

C   We really don't know when ice cream was invented, but it's likely the first people who made something like ice cream were in China around the seventh or eighth century. They used milk from cows, buffalo or goats, and put it into ice pools in metal tubes to freeze it, then served it to emperors.

15 AUGUST

B   A woodpecker can peck around 20 times a second! It has extra muscles in its skull that work like a helmet to protect its brain from jiggling around when it's busy pecking.

16 AUGUST

B   Hummingbirds drink more than their own body weight in nectar each day. They do this with their long thin beaks and long tongues that stick out of their beaks. The nectar gives them energy to fly from flower to flower, drinking nectar, and as they do this they also spread pollen around for the plants. Thousands of flower species rely on hummingbirds to spread their pollen!

17 AUGUST

A The kākāpō is a flightless parrot found only in New Zealand. Its Māori name means "night parrot", because it is nocturnal and only comes out at night. It also happens to be the heaviest parrot in the world, with the males weighing up to 2.2 kilograms. These round-faced green birds are full of personality! They might not be able to fly, but they're excellent climbers and pretty good at walking, too. And, when it's time to breed, the males put on a show to find a mate: they create a "bowl" in the ground, then sit in it and make a deep booming noise every couple of seconds, trying to attract a female. Kākāpō are critically endangered, with only around 240 currently remaining, but people are working hard to protect them and save them from extinction.

18 AUGUST

A + B Aye-ayes are primates that live in the forests of Madagascar, an island off the southeastern coast of Africa. They use their long fingers to find food by tapping on wood to make sounds that help them to find bugs hiding inside trees. They also use their fingers to pick their noses!

19 AUGUST

B Philosophers and scientists have struggled to explain exactly why we cry when we feel emotions, such as being happy or sad. When babies cry, they often do it for attention, as they can't express themselves with words – and adults might do this, too! There are lots of reasons why we cry, and it's good to cry when you need to.

20 AUGUST

C When we sleep, our tongues, mouths, throats and noses relax. For some of us, the air moving through these body parts makes them vibrate, and it sounds like a snore. You're more likely to snore when you sleep on your back!

21 AUGUST

C There are more than 12,000 species of ant in the world. Ants live on every continent, except Antarctica.

22 AUGUST

A A fly's wings are made from cuticle, as are its legs and joints. Cuticle is the second most common natural material in the world, and it's much tougher than bone. It is also bendy, and is a bit like our fingernails.

23 AUGUST

C   At top speed, honeybees can fly up to 20 miles (32 kilometres) per hour – that's about as fast as a squirrel. They go slower on their way back to the hive, when they are laden with pollen – around 12 miles (19 kilometres) per hour.

24 AUGUST

C   Mauna Kea is a volcano on the island of Hawai'i that rises 4,207.3 metres above sea level – but, if you measure it from its under-sea base, it's actually about 9,966 metres tall! This makes it about 1,116 metres taller than Mount Everest (also known as Chomolungma or Sagarmāthā) in the Himalaya.

25 AUGUST

C   Studies of Mount Etna in Sicily, in Italy, suggest the volcano has been active for about 2.6 million years, making it Europe's most active volcano. Mount Etna was already very old when its first recorded eruption took place in 1500 BCE, and since then it has erupted at least 200 more times.

26 AUGUST

C According to Guinness World Records, the longest river in the world is the Nile – but, according to others, the Amazon is longer! The Nile stretches 4,160 miles (6,695 kilometres) from its main source, Lake Victoria in east central Africa, to its farthest stream, in Burundi. The Amazon, however, is hard to measure accurately, because scientists argue over its start and end points.

27 AUGUST

A An octopus shoots out ink to escape from, confuse and scare away predators. The ink comes from a sac inside the octopus's body, and is mixed with mucus before the octopus shoots it into the water. Sometimes, the ink is in clouds or trails, and other times it's octopus-shaped!

28 AUGUST

B An octopus has two eyes which can move in different directions.

29 AUGUST

C An octopus has three hearts: two to pump blood to its gills, and a third to pump blood round its body.

30 AUGUST

C   A seahorse swims using a small fin on its back that flutters up to 35 times per second. Seahorses are the slowest-moving of all fish.

31 AUGUST

A   Octopuses and squids are carnivorous, which means they eat meat rather than plants. They use their beaks to kill and chop up the sea creatures that are their food.

1 SEPTEMBER

A   Burps happen when gas from your stomach escapes through your mouth. The sound is made by the gas vibrating your vocal cords, and changes depending on how much gas comes out, and how forcefully. Farts happen when gas comes out of your intestines through your bottom! The sound changes depending on the speed of the gas, how tight the muscles in your bottom are, and whether or not there is poo in your intestines waiting to come out.

2 SEPTEMBER

C   Wee and poo go down a sewerage pipe, then join with wee, poo and waste from other houses and buildings. This mixture of waste is called sewage. It then goes into bigger sewerage pipes, some of which are even bigger than a bus! The sewage flowing through them is like a river. It all goes to a treatment plant, which is like a big factory where the sewage is cleaned. Then, once the harmful stuff is taken out, it goes into the sea or a local river.

3 SEPTEMBER

C   The word checkmate comes from the Persian word *shah mat*, which means "the King is dead". The quickest a player can checkmate their

opponent is in two moves, and the longest
a game can take is (in theory) 5,949 moves.

4 SEPTEMBER

C In 1931, New York City architect Alfred Mosher
Butts invented Scrabble. He added up the
letters on the front page of *The New York Times*
newspaper to work out how frequently they were
used, and how much a letter should be worth. At
first, he called the game Lexico, then Criss-Cross
Words, and finally Scrabble!

5 SEPTEMBER

B The highest score you can get in Scrabble is
1,782 points with OXYPHENBUTAZONE.
In order to get this many points, the word
would have to be played across the top of the
board, using three Triple Word Score squares,
while making seven crosswords downwards.
CAZIQUES with 392 points is the highest-scoring
word ever played in a real game so far.

6 SEPTEMBER

A Snakes and Ladders was invented in India a long
time ago. It was called Mokshapat or Moksha
Patamu, and was played around the second
century BCE. The game was meant to teach

children about good behaviour (virtue) and doing naughty things (evil). The ladders were virtue, and the snakes evil. The game was brought to England in the nineteenth century, and the teachings about virtue and evil were taken out.

7 SEPTEMBER

A Archaeologists believe that the oldest known carpet was made in Armenia. It is known as the Pazyryk rug, and was made by hand around 2,500 years ago, but is still almost perfectly intact with glowing colours of red, green and gold.

8 SEPTEMBER

C Yoga was invented in northern India over 5,000 years ago. The word yoga first appeared in an ancient Indian text called the *Rig Veda*, which was written in Sanskrit.

9 SEPTEMBER

A As far as we can tell, the Sumerians may have been the first people to develop a system of writing. It was called cuneiform, and was written on wet clay, using a reed as a pen. Once the writing was finished, the clay tablet was baked in the Sun, then given to others to read.

10 SEPTEMBER

A   Paper as we know it today was first made in China, some time around the year 105. An imperial court official created a sheet of paper using mulberry and other plant fibres, along with fishnets, old rags and hemp waste.

11 SEPTEMBER

B   We aren't sure what causes a stitch. One theory is that, when you run, your stomach and liver pull on the little things called ligaments which connect them to the diaphragm, the muscle that separates the stomach from the heart and lungs. Some scientists think eating a big meal right before exercising causes bad digestion, which could lead to a stitch.

12 SEPTEMBER

C   Blue whales have the loudest call of any creature on Earth – it can reach 188 decibels, which is as loud as a jet plane! Much smaller, but just as loud, is the tiny tiger pistol shrimp, which doesn't have a call but does make a bubble with its claw that causes a shockwave that can reach more than 200 decibels.

13 SEPTEMBER

B Mammals are warm-blooded, and need a high body temperature to survive. Hair and fur trap air around their bodies, which keeps them warm and insulates them against the cold. The thicker the hair or fur, the warmer their bodies will be.

14 SEPTEMBER

B When mucus, dirt and bacteria dry out and clump together inside your nose, you're left with a bogey.

15 SEPTEMBER

C When you feel stressed, hot or embarrassed and your cheeks go red, it's called blushing. Strong feelings send messages of stress to the nervous system, which tells your face muscles to relax. This causes the blood vessels to widen and more blood flows to the skin, which makes your face turn red.

16 SEPTEMBER

C Toenails keep the blood vessels, muscles and flesh underneath them safe. They're a bit like armour for the tips of your toes!

17 SEPTEMBER

A   Cats can see much better in dim light than humans can, as they have more cells that detect light in their eyes, but they don't see as many colours as we do. Vibrant colours look more like pastels to cats, and they have trouble distinguishing between green and red.

18 SEPTEMBER

B   Cats like to be nice and clean, but wet fur doesn't feel nice. It also takes ages to dry, and is heavy and weighs a cat down when it's running about. There are some cats, however, that *do* like playing with water. Breeds such as Maine Coons and Bengals love it so much they'll play and splash around in it any opportunity they get, and will even try to get in the shower with you if you're not careful!

19 SEPTEMBER

A   Most cats do have eyelashes! They're just tricky to see with all the fur on a cat's face. A cat's eyelashes are called cilia, and they line the upper and lower parts of the eyelid.

ANSWERS

20 SEPTEMBER

A   The most likely reason for a lynx's ear tufts is to direct sound into its ears, helping them to hear better and find their prey more easily.

21 SEPTEMBER

B   Although they look similar, jaguars are more muscular than leopards, with a wider head and big, strong jaws. Leopards are nimbler at climbing trees, and have longer tails, which help them balance. In the wild, they also live on different continents. Jaguars live in Central and South America, while leopards are found in China, parts of Russia and India, the Middle East and down into Africa.

22 SEPTEMBER

A   Unlike mammals, birds don't wee. But seagulls do a lot of white poo! One study also found that birds are most likely to poo on red cars, followed by blue and black – but it really depends on where you park.

23 SEPTEMBER

A   Birds mostly sleep high up in trees, either on the upper branches or in holes in the tree. They also sleep in gutters, birdhouses, chimneys and small caves – anywhere out of reach of predators. Birds only sleep in nests when they have eggs or chicks to care for.

24 SEPTEMBER

C Between 1968 and 1972, the United States of America sent several Apollo missions to the Moon. On these, 24 astronauts flew into the Moon's orbit, but only twelve actually walked on it.

25 SEPTEMBER

A The stars are always there, but in the daytime we can't see them because the light of the Sun is so strong it blocks out their light. When the Sun sets at night, we can see the light from other stars.

26 SEPTEMBER

B Sundials were some of the earliest technology used to tell time. They have a dial with markings on it, and a part called a gnomon which casts a shadow. When the Sun shines on a dial, the gnomon casts a shadow – and where the shadow lands on the dial depends on where in the sky the Sun is. As the Sun's position in our sky changes during the day, the shadow cast moves clockwise round the dial. So, when clocks were being made in mediaeval times, their hands were made to spin the same way as the shadow on a sundial.

27 SEPTEMBER

B If you insert a silver wire and a copper wire in it, a single lemon becomes a kind of battery and can produce 0.7 volts (seven tenths of a volt) of electricity. Connect the wires from two lemons, and you can make about 1.5 volts – that's enough to power a cheap digital watch!

28 SEPTEMBER

A Flying fish can't exactly fly, but they do glide! To do so, they swim fast underwater, then leap out of the water and use their fins to glide through the air. They can glide around 50 metres through the air like this – and, if they catch the edge of a wave, they can use the wave to glide for up to 200 metres! There are more than 70 species of flying fish, so the height they glide at varies. Baby flying fish have whiskers near their mouths that camouflage them by making them look like plant blossoms.

29 SEPTEMBER

C Lots of turtle and tortoise species can pull
their heads into their shells, but sea turtles can't.
They have smaller, flatter shells that help them
to move fast, and flipper-like feet that make
them speedy swimmers. So, they can't hide in
their shells from predators, but they can get
away quickly!

30 SEPTEMBER

C Dolphins have really smooth and soft skin
because the outer layer can come off and be
replaced by new skin cells every two hours! This is
probably to make the dolphins really fast in the
water – it means no bits of skin stick out to slow
them down as they swim.

1 OCTOBER

B   The fur on the end of a lion's tail is called a tail tuft! A lion uses it to communicate with other lions. The tuft is darker than the lion's body fur, so other lions can see it, and the lion can use it to lead them through long grass.

2 OCTOBER

A   Male lions have manes to show how fit and strong they are, and female lions like males with big dark manes! Their manes also protect their necks and throats from getting hurt when they're fighting other lions.

3 OCTOBER

C   The tiger pistol shrimp's claws shoot jets of water that move so quickly they make an air bubble which, when it bursts, creates a shock wave louder than a blue whale's song. It's so loud it can even kill nearby fish! Luckily, the tiger pistol shrimp lives underwater, otherwise the sounds it makes would burst our eardrums!

4 OCTOBER

C   The biggest predatory cat, the Siberian tiger, can be 3 metres long and weigh up to 300 kilograms.

5 OCTOBER

C   A googolplex is thought to be the biggest number in the world. It is so large that we cannot write it in normal number format!

6 OCTOBER

A   The official name of China's currency is the renminbi, meaning "the people's money" – but the yuan is a unit of this currency, so that is often used instead.

7 OCTOBER

C   Freyr is Freya's brother in Norse mythology. He is the ruler of peace and fertility, rain and sunshine.

8 OCTOBER

B   The Denmark Strait is a HUGE waterfall under the Atlantic Ocean, between Greenland and Iceland. What? Under the ocean? Yes! The water in the Denmark Strait has cold water on one side, and warm water on the other – and, when the two waters mix, the cold water sinks. This makes a waterfall that is the same size as 2,000 of the biggest waterfalls above the ocean, and it falls for 3,505 metres!

9 OCTOBER

C   Praia do Cassino in Brazil is the longest beach in the world. It stretches up to 158 miles (254 kilometres) from the entrance of the Rio Grande seaport, in Brazil, all the way south to the border with Uruguay.

10 OCTOBER

A   Oysters make pearls when something annoying gets into their shell, and they coat it with something called nacre. This is usually a worm, but oyster farmers who are growing pearls might deliberately put a bead in the shell for the pearl to grow around.

11 OCTOBER

C   Hydrogen is the lightest element in the universe, and also the element that there is the most of! It has no colour or smell, and makes up 10 per cent of the human body and 90 per cent of all known atoms in the universe.

12 OCTOBER

A There is gravity everywhere, even in space.

13 OCTOBER

C Stars are made of hot gases, mostly hydrogen and helium.

14 OCTOBER

C The *Saturn V* was built by the National Aeronautics and Space Administration (NASA) to send astronauts to the Moon on its Apollo space missions, and was 111 metres tall. The first one took off in 1967, and the last in 1973, when it launched the Skylab, the first American space station.

15 OCTOBER

B The biggest popcorn machine in the world is at a theme park in Phuket, an island in Thailand. It is 7.89 metres tall, 3.53 metres wide and 2.83 metres deep, and can make four flavours of popcorn at once: extreme cheese, praline chocolate, island salt and crème caramel.

16 OCTOBER

B   To make butter, fresh milk is first separated into skimmed milk and cream. The cream is then churned, or mixed around, for long enough that little lumps begin to form. These lumps are butter, and if you keep churning the lumps get bigger. They are formed by the fat in the cream breaking open and sticking together as butter.

17 OCTOBER

B   Some sparkling water comes out of the Earth lightly sparkling. However, to make extra-bubbly sparkling water, carbon dioxide is added to still water.

18 OCTOBER

A   The word pacific means peaceful, and the ocean was given that name by Portuguese sailor Ferdinand Magellan – he called it *Mar Pacífico*, which means "peaceful sea" in Portuguese. It is the largest ocean on the planet and the deepest, and it's not always peaceful. Sometimes, it can be quite stormy! It also has several other names that have been used by Pacific peoples for centuries – since long before Magellan ever turned up there – including *Moananuiākea* (Hawaiian) and *Te-moana-nui-a-Kiwa* (Māori).

19 OCTOBER

B Whales sing beautiful songs that can travel for thousands of miles through the ocean. In the vast underwater space of the ocean, sound travels four times faster than it does in air, so whales use song to talk to each other across long distances.

20 OCTOBER

B When scientists lowered an underwater microphone, called a hydrophone, to the bottom of the Mariana Trench – the deepest part of the ocean – they heard earthquakes, whale song and other sounds!

21 OCTOBER

A Sharks have no bones in their bodies! Their skeletons are made of cartilage, which is lighter than bone.

22 OCTOBER

C The animal that lives longer than any other on Earth is the clam! A type of clam called an ocean quahog was found in Iceland in 2006 that was 507 years old – scientists worked out its age by counting the rings, called growth bands, in its shell.

23 OCTOBER

B   The elf owl is the smallest in the world, and lives in the southwestern United States of America and in northern Mexico. It sometimes lives in saguaro, giant tree-like cactuses, where it nests in little holes made by other animals. It can also make a home on telegraph poles or in trees.

24 OCTOBER

B   A few species of owl are active during the day. The long-legged burrowing owl in North and South America nests in the ground, and lives in tunnels made by other animals, such as prairie dogs. During the day, it sits at the entrance to its home alongside piles of poo! Why? Because the poo attracts dung beetles, which the owl loves to eat. Cowboys used to call these owls howdy birds, because they look like they're nodding "hello" when they're sitting outside their homes.

25 OCTOBER

A   All three of these answers are reasons why
+   a tractor has big wheels and small wheels.
B   A tractor's large back wheels have better grip
+   on the muddy ground – this is important,
C   because tractors are usually pulling heavy things behind them, so there's a risk of the back wheels being pulled down into the mud.

A bigger wheel means the tyre can bite into the ground, rather than sinking into it. The height also helps the tractor driver to see the field they're working on, and the smaller front wheels are much better at steering round sharp corners.

26 OCTOBER

A The world's fastest public train is the maglev that runs between Shanghai Pudong International Airport and a station in central Shanghai. It can travel at 268 miles (431 kilometres) per hour.

27 OCTOBER

B Whales rest in the water by hanging vertically or horizontally, or they sleep while swimming slowly next to another whale.

28 OCTOBER

B Most mammals have seven bones in their necks – including you! Whales haves seven bones in their necks, and so do giraffes! The bones are just different lengths!

29 OCTOBER

B The bumblebee bat, also known as the Kitti's hog-nosed bat, is the smallest in the world. It weighs just 2 grams!

30 OCTOBER

B Our bones support our bodies – we couldn't stand or walk or do anything without the bones that make up our skeleton. Bones also protect the organs in our bodies. Our skulls protect our brains, and create all of our differently shaped faces. Bones also hold bone marrow, which is where we make red blood cells (which carry oxygen around our bodies), white blood cells (which fight off germs) and platelets (which stop you bleeding if you hurt yourself).

31 OCTOBER

B Children have carved vegetables – first turnips, then pumpkins – to look like spirits, then lit them with candles at Halloween for thousands of years to scare away ghosts.

1 NOVEMBER

A Diwali means "row of lights" in Sanskrit, an ancient language in India. It is known as the Festival of Lights, and it is celebrated around the world by 800 million people! At Diwali, we light oil lamps and put them in our houses and gardens. These lights, called diyas, symbolize throwing out darkness and evil, and bringing in light and goodness to celebrate the New Year. We also set off fireworks, swap presents and make delicious food.

2 NOVEMBER

A Camels spit to surprise, distract or scare away anything they feel is bothering them. Camel spit isn't like your spit – it's more like vomit. They bring up what's in their stomach, along with saliva, and spit it all out. So, if you see a camel's cheeks filling up, run! It's about to spit!

3 NOVEMBER

B According to Guinness World Records, the longest non-stop dance party ever was held in Beirut, in Lebanon, in 2017, and went on for 56 hours! Before that, the longest dance party was a 55-hour boogie-fest in Ireland, in 2006.

4 NOVEMBER

B Glass is made by heating sand (or soda ash, or limestone) until it gets so hot it melts and turns into something new! At first, the melted sand is a liquid, but when it cools it is glass – and can be turned into lots of different things, including windows, vases and even sunglasses!

5 NOVEMBER

C Blue cheese gets its smell (and colour) from a type of mould called penicillium. It isn't covered in mould because it has gone off – instead, the cheesemaker puts it there because some people love the flavour! Cheesemakers inject the mould into the cheese, and it's the mould that makes the cheese stinky.

6 NOVEMBER

C On average, people in the United Kingdom eat 30 grams of cheese a day, which amounts to more than 10 kilograms a year! As of 2019, the countries that ate the most cheese per person were the Czech Republic, Germany and France.

7 NOVEMBER

C   German blue rams are fish that come from South America. The males are yellow-green with blue dots, and they're named after Manuel Ramirez, one of their first collectors.

8 NOVEMBER

B   When a huge asteroid hit the Earth 66 million years ago, it caused earthquakes, giant waves, volcanic eruptions and landslides across the planet, which caused many dinosaurs to die. But it was the dust, ash and smoke caused by the asteroid crash that eventually led to all the dinosaurs becoming extinct, because it blocked out the Sun's light for years and changed the Earth's climate. Plants couldn't survive without light, so they died. This meant the plant-eating dinosaurs that had survived the asteroid crash had nothing to eat, so they ended up dying, too. Then, the meat-eating dinosaurs had no plant eaters to eat, so they died as well. And that's how the dinosaurs became extinct.

9 NOVEMBER

B   The *barosaurus* was a huge 15-metre-tall dinosaur, and scientists think it had eight hearts – probably so that it could pump blood all the way up its really long neck to its brain.

10 NOVEMBER

C   Researchers aren't sure of the exact lifespan of
blobfish because these creatures live so deep in
the ocean. However, it's thought that blobfish live
for more than 100 years (possibly up to 130 years)
because they don't have predators, and because
they grow slowly.

11 NOVEMBER

A   Tigers can have around 100 stripes on their fur.
The Grévy's zebra is the stripiest zebra, with
about 80 stripes. Chipmunks have only four or
five stripes on their body.

12 NOVEMBER

C   Giraffes hum to each other at night, but we can't
hear it as the sound is too low for our ears to
pick up. During the day, they make moans and
grunts. Giraffes also communicate by using their
eyes and touching one another.

13 NOVEMBER

C   Sperm whales have the largest brain of any
living animal. Their brains can weigh up to
9 kilograms – that's as heavy as a watermelon!

14 NOVEMBER

B   Hippos release something called "blood sweat", which is pinkish because it has pigments in it that help to protect the hippos' skin. Blood sweat stops their skin from getting sunburnt or drying out, keeps them at a good temperature and fights bacteria.

15 NOVEMBER

A   Scientists think that ants are one of the most intelligent insects, and have the largest brains of all insects.

16 NOVEMBER

A   *Gauromydas heros*, the world's biggest fly, can have a body as long as 7 centimetres and a wingspan of around 10 centimetres. They live in Brazil, Bolivia and Paraguay.

17 NOVEMBER

B   Spiders have tiny triangular hairs on their feet. When they touch a wall, they make a temporary force – called a van der Waals force – that sticks them to it. They can even change the angle the hairs stick at, to help them walk along.

18 NOVEMBER

C Snails usually come out at night, but will pop out during the day if it has been raining. They do this to avoid drying out, as they use up lots of water when they make slime. When it's hot, snails stay in their shells to keep moist.

19 NOVEMBER

B The biggest stick insect is *Phobaeticus kirbyi* of Borneo. It is over 53 centimetres long with its legs stretched out, and is one of the world's largest insects.

20 NOVEMBER

B Lightning is an electrical release caused by imbalances between storm clouds and the ground, or within the clouds themselves. During a storm, the clouds get a negative charge from the particles of rain, ice or snow inside them, while objects on the ground such as trees gain a positive charge. The difference between these charges causes lightning to be released to bring things back into balance.

21 NOVEMBER

A The Sun makes light, also called solar radiation. Solar panels have little cells, called photovoltaic cells, that take this light and turn it into energy, or electricity.

22 NOVEMBER

A Magnets produce a magnetic field around them because of the way the particles in the material are aligned. This can act as a force on other things – especially other magnets.

23 NOVEMBER

A The world's largest wolf is the Mackenzie Valley wolf, which can weigh around 70 kilograms and be up to 2 metres long.

24 NOVEMBER

C The Latin name for a red fox is *Vulpes vulpes*, which technically means "fox fox"!

25 NOVEMBER

C Nocturnal animals tend to have big eyes, as well as cells that can pick up scattered and dim light. Some even have a mirror-like layer in their eyes that makes the most of any light there is by reflecting it within the eye.

26 NOVEMBER

B Orangutans, gorillas, chimpanzees and bonobos respond to being tickled by laughing, just like humans do. Dogs, meerkats and even rats seem to enjoy being tickled, too.

27 NOVEMBER

A Diamonds on jewellery shine because they are cut to give them many surfaces, called facets. When light reflects off these facets, the diamonds sparkle.

28 NOVEMBER

C Cement is made by first extracting raw materials, such as limestone and clay, from quarries, then crushing and mixing them together, before finally heating the mixture in big ovens.

29 NOVEMBER

C Falcon Nest in Prescott, Arizona, in the United States of America, is the world's tallest single-family home. It was designed by architect Sukumar Pal, and is 10 storeys high and 38 metres tall.

30 NOVEMBER

B Skyscrapers – the tall, modern buildings you see in cities – came about in the 1880s. The word skyscraper was first used to describe buildings that had 10 to 20 platforms or storeys, but now it means buildings with more than 40 floors. The Burj Khalifa in Dubai has 163!

ANSWERS

1 DECEMBER

B   Penguins drink seawater as they swim, and they have a special gland in their bodies that can filter salt out of their bloodstream. The salt comes out of their nostrils, which is why penguins often have a sniffly nose and shake their heads a lot – it's all the salt coming out!

2 DECEMBER

C   The Antarctic midge is the only species of insect that lives in Antarctica. It is a tiny 2–6-millimetre fly, and has no wings so it doesn't get blown away.

3 DECEMBER

A   Penguins' beaks are made of keratin, a strong material we have in our fingernails and birds have in their claws.

4 DECEMBER

A   Penguins look carefully at one another's beaks when deciding who to have baby penguins with. Good penguin pairs have similar beak colours!

5 DECEMBER

C   Polar bears' bodies are designed for walking in the Arctic. They have huge paws that are 30 centimetres across – the size of dinner plates – and have black pads on the bottom that are covered in little bumps called papillae. These bumps grip the ice, and stop the bears from slipping in the snow.

6 DECEMBER

C   Icicles form when melted ice or snow drips down and refreezes because the air temperature is below freezing. One drop of water freezes, then the next drop freezes on top of it, and so on, until an icicle eventually forms.

7 DECEMBER

B   Hyenas make a noise that sounds like laughter when they are in conflict, for instance when fighting for food. This sound shows that they're frustrated, they're under attack or one of their pack has just made a kill. It also shows their social status.

8 DECEMBER

B   An elephant's ears are thin and filled with tiny blood vessels that help it to cool down.

9 DECEMBER

C Alligators and crocodiles are both in the *Crocodilia* group of species, but they have many differences. Crocodiles have pointier snouts, more visible teeth, greener colouring, and are more aggressive than alligators. They also tend to prefer saltwater, while alligators favour freshwater.

10 DECEMBER

C Only one in every 10,000 clover plants will have four leaves, which is why it's so hard to find one! The Latin name for clover is *Trifolium*, which means "three leaves", and clovers with four leaves have a mutation in their make-up. Sometimes you can find clovers with even more leaves – the record number is 56, found in Japan in 2009.

11 DECEMBER

A Mushrooms live for only a few weeks, but they are just the fruiting part of a bigger organism called a fungus. The underground fungal networks that create mushrooms can live for thousands of years. A honey fungus in the Blue Mountains of Oregon, in the United States of America, is estimated to be around 2,000 years old – but scientists say it could be as old as 8,650 years!

12 DECEMBER

A Based on the amount of the plant it would take to kill a human, the castor oil plant is the deadliest. It would take 70 micrograms of castor bean to kill an adult – that's up to eight of its tiny seeds!

13 DECEMBER

B The Olmecs lived long ago in what is now Central America, and were the first people to make chocolate. They prepared a chocolate drink with cacao beans that they used for rituals and as medicine. Hundreds of years later, the people of the Maya civilization, in what is now southeastern Mexico, cultivated the cacao plant for food and saw it as a sacred gift from the gods. It was a while before this drink was made into a hard chocolate, like chocolate bars, however.

14 DECEMBER

B The Formula Rossa rollercoaster in Abu Dhabi, in the United Arab Emirates, gives you the thrill of feeling like you're driving in a Formula One car. It accelerates to a speed of 149 miles (240 kilometres) per hour in just a few seconds. Strap in!

15 DECEMBER

B   Human-like remote-controlled robots were developed in the 1920s, but the first digitally operated and programmable robot was created in the 1950s by American inventor George Devol for use in factories and other businesses that make things.

16 DECEMBER

B   Shoes don't fossilize like bodies do, so it's very difficult to tell when they might have been invented. The oldest shoes we know of are a collection of bark sandals found in Fort Rock Cave, in Oregon, in the United States of America. They date from 10,000 BCE to 7,000 BCE, making them at least 9,000 years old.

17 DECEMBER

C   Yawning is a bit of a mystery! Scientists used to think that we yawned partly to take in more oxygen when we were tired, but that's now believed to be unlikely. Instead, more recent research suggests that yawning may make us more alert, and also helps to cool our brain down. Plus yawning is catching!

18 DECEMBER

C   When your body digests food, it creates gases in your intestines. You also swallow air while you're eating and drinking. These gases need to be released, so they come out in the form of a fart – or a burp!

19 DECEMBER

B   Blood cells are made in the bone marrow, which is the soft, spongy material in the centre of our bones.

20 DECEMBER

A   Robins usually have two legs.

21 DECEMBER

C   Fir trees have been used in winter festivals for millennia. In Germany in the 1500s, families began putting candles on the trees. Later, they used gingerbread, sweets, paper decorations and baubles. This tradition came to England when King George III married Princess Charlotte from Germany. She loved Christmas trees and threw a big party for children with a tree to remind her of home, and soon everyone wanted one!

22 DECEMBER

B In Victorian times, Royal Mail postmen in the United Kingdom wore bright red coats, so were nicknamed "robin redbreasts". Christmas cards became popular during this time, and because they were delivered by postmen, people began drawing robins on them.

23 DECEMBER

A + B Different types of trees, such as spruce, fir and pines, are used for Christmas. They can take between six and ten years to grow and up to fifteen years for taller trees!

24 DECEMBER

B Saint Nicholas was the patron saint of children, and was known for giving them gifts. He was the original Father Christmas, or Santa Claus!

25 DECEMBER

C An English sweet maker called Tom Smith invented Christmas crackers about 170 years ago. The story goes that he got the idea for the *crack!* while watching logs crackling in his fireplace!

26 DECEMBER

B   It's unlikely you'll ever see two snowflakes that are the same shape. The idea that no two snowflakes are the same comes from a farmer in the United States of America called Wilson "Snowflake" Bentley, who was the first person to photograph snowflakes close up. He took photos of more than 5,000 snowflakes, and each one looked different. There are thought to be about a million flakes in 1 litre of snow, and snow has been falling for billions of years, so there probably have been some snowflakes that *are* alike – but the chances of actually seeing two the same are tiny!

27 DECEMBER

C   When the blades of a helicopter are spinning very fast, they are pushing the air over the top of the helicopter faster than the air is being pushed under it. This means there is less air pressure on top of the blades, which creates the force of "lift" – so the helicopter moves upwards!

28 DECEMBER

A   Electricity begins with an energy source, such as fossil fuels, the wind or the Sun. Big power stations catch the energy from these sources and turn it into electricity, which is then spread far and wide to power our toasters and our kettles.

29 DECEMBER

C   Inside a microwave oven, there's a device called a magnetron that sends out microwaves that go into the food. These "microwaves" make the water inside the food vibrate, which makes heat, which cooks the food!

30 DECEMBER

C   It takes approximately 365.2422 days for the Earth to complete a full orbit of the Sun, so we make a year 365 days to be about the same as the orbit. We save up the extra little bit of orbit (0.2422 days!) at the end of the year and use it every four years to make one extra day in February. This is called a leap year, and the extra day is 29 February. Doing this brings the year closer to being the length of the Earth's orbit round the Sun.

31 DECEMBER

B   The Oxford English Dictionary, in its second edition (1989), contained 171,476 words in current use, as well as 47,156 words that were obsolete. That's a lot compared with some other European languages!

ARTISTS

Thank you to the talented artists
who illustrated the pages and
brought this book to life:

Momoko Abe

Alice Courtley

Kelsey Buzzell

Sandra De La Prada

Beatrice Cerocchi

Grace Easton

Manuela Montoya Escobar

Gwen Millward

Richard Jones

Sally Mullaney

Lisa Koesterke

Laurie Stansfield